TRIBAL FARMERS AND NEW AGRICULTURAL TECHNOLOGY

TRIBAL FARMERS AND NEW AGRICULTURAL TECHNOLOGY

BHOLA NATH GHOSH

AKANSHA PUBLISHING HOUSE
NEW DELHI

AKANSHA PUBLISHING HOUSE
4649/21B, Ansari Road
Darya Ganj
New Delhi - 110 002
Ph.: 23263193 / 9811582579
E-mail:ektabooks@yahoo.com

Tribal Farmers and New Agricultural Technology

First Published 2005
ISBN 81-8370-026-8

[The responsibility for the facts stated, conclusions reached etc. is entirely that of the Author. The publisher is not responsible for them, whatsoever.]

PRINTED IN INDIA

Published by M.P. Misra for Akansha Publishing House, New Delhi and Printed at Tarun Offset Press, Delhi.

FOREWORD

India is a country where about 40 per cent of its total population perpetually live below poverty line. In such a situation of abject poverty, planning needs are to be oriented to be more manpower investing than capital investing. During the past few Five-Year Plans of our country, this fact seems to engage very little attention of our planning, especially in respect of the rural sector where agricultural innovating have been pressed into farmer's services without assessing its possible dysfunction. As a result the lot of the several landless and land poor agricultural farmers have further worsened because the new agricultural technology is hardly suitable to meet their ends and the gap between the landless poor and the landed gentry has further widened.

Therefore, this human problem requires investigation regarding the long-term socio-economic consequences of adoption of technological innovation in respect of people especially the "Tribal people" who have largely become the victims of the development process. Technology, for them, instead of becoming a source of empowerment, has become a source of further deprivation.

In India where the problem of population growth is assuming alarming form, no technological innovations could be adopted at the cost of the worsening socio-economic conditions of the destitute sections of our people i.e. mainly the tribal people.

The goals of diffusion and dissemination of research should principally identify the process by which agricultural innovations diffuse within villages and the factors, which influence their adoption by tribal farmers.

The present study points out that the methodology followed in many previous studies to consider innovation adoption in dichotomous terms (adoption/non-adoption) may be the appropriate in many cases where the actual decisions may be more appropriately in terms of continuous range (such as package to be used).

This study can be identified as an attempt to identify the cumulative impact of certain major factors contributing to the process of adoption of new technology in the study area. It has been found that the amount of land holding is of prime importance for adopting new technologies in agriculture. For the households as a whole of whom majority is small and marginal farmers, the effect of sex, age, education and family size are marginal and only the land holding size becomes the major factor.

The author has analysed the data by the application of sophisticated statistical tool i.e. multivariate analysis. This analysis shows that while the partial effects of all the variables come to play important role, the synergic effect is what matters and that is what has to be analysed in order to make a specific explanation. It is also observed that family structure like nuclear family or joint family has no specific effect in causing motivation. Literacy as such is not that important unless combined with other factors. Most of the farmers become aware of the new idea of technology in agriculture through friends, neighbours and kins. But marginal farmers generally do not want to take any risk involved in adopting the new technology.

The study also indicates that the farmers in the "small" category (as distinguished from the marginal ones) have responded well like the "large" ones. Because their economic-status has allowed them to make experimentation with the new technologies.

The study also shows that higher number in packages, higher in the rate of adoption. It can be argued that as the number in the packages increases the cost of the packages escalates. Therefore, the marginal farmers allege against the "costly practice". The author claimed that closer the source of propagators of modern technologies, greater will be the rate of adoption.

Therefore, the findings of this study are expected to be of use for the extension workers working in rural areas in their endeavour to accelerate the rate of adoption of agricultural innovations by farmers. This type of study has also become an important part of the curricula for students in rural sociology.

Prof. Swapan Kumar Pramanick
Vice-Chancellor of Vidyasagar University,
West Midnapore,
West Bengal

PREFACE

This research on adoption behaviour of tribal cultivators was undertaken by me almost a decade. The report was submitted to the Indian Statistical Institute in 1994. The subject earned my interest as I was also working as a member of Indian Statistical Institute evaluation team on Rain-Fed Farming in Eastern Indian States.

Recently, I attended a conference on sustainable agriculture where adoption of technology was one of the much-discussed subjects. I presented the results of this study in the conference as to how tribal farmers behave in the matter of adoption of technology, which aroused interest among the fellow participants. Some of my seniors and many younger scholars suggested me not to allow this report to gather dust as it would be of much use to the young research workers and students in the field of agrarian and anthropological research.

This study was made possible by research grant provided by Social Science Division of Indian Statistical Institute, Kolkata. I am grateful to my Institute and the Divisional Committee of Scientific Workers in Social Science for rendering material support for this study.

I express my gratitude to Prof. Atis Dasgupta, Prof. Suraj Bandyopadhayay, Prof. Biswanath Bhattacharya, Late Prof. Asok Maiti, Prof. A. R. Rao, Prof. Bikas Sinha and Prof. Manoranjan Pal of Indian Statistical Institute,

Kolkata, Dr. S.B. Chakraborti, retired Deputy Director, Anthropological Survey of India and Prof. Donald Van Eschen, Department of Sociology, Mcgill University, Canada for their creative suggestion, constructive comments and encouragement.

I thank Dr. Santanu Mukherjee, Dr. Tapan Sasmal, Dr. Debashis Bhattcharjee, Dr. Tirthankar Ghosh, Shri Partha De and Shri Rabindra Nath Jana to help in different times to preparing this manuscript and all the other of my colleagues of Sociological Research Unit at the Indian Statistical Institute for their understanding and kindness.

I am greatly indebted to the villagers of Kabilpur, Latapakur and Bamundiha for their attention and kind cooperation, which enabled me to conduct this study and without whose cooperation I would not have written a line.

I hope, this would be of some use to student and research workers who are interested in studying human behaviour in adoption of technology for changing the standard and quality of life and living. My labour in this work would be amply rewarded if this hope is fulfilled.

I, therefore, decided to publish this and I am grateful that Akansha Publishing House has kindly agreed to publish it.

Bhola Nath Ghosh

CONTENTS

LIST OF TABLES

LIST OF MAPS

LIST OF FIGURES

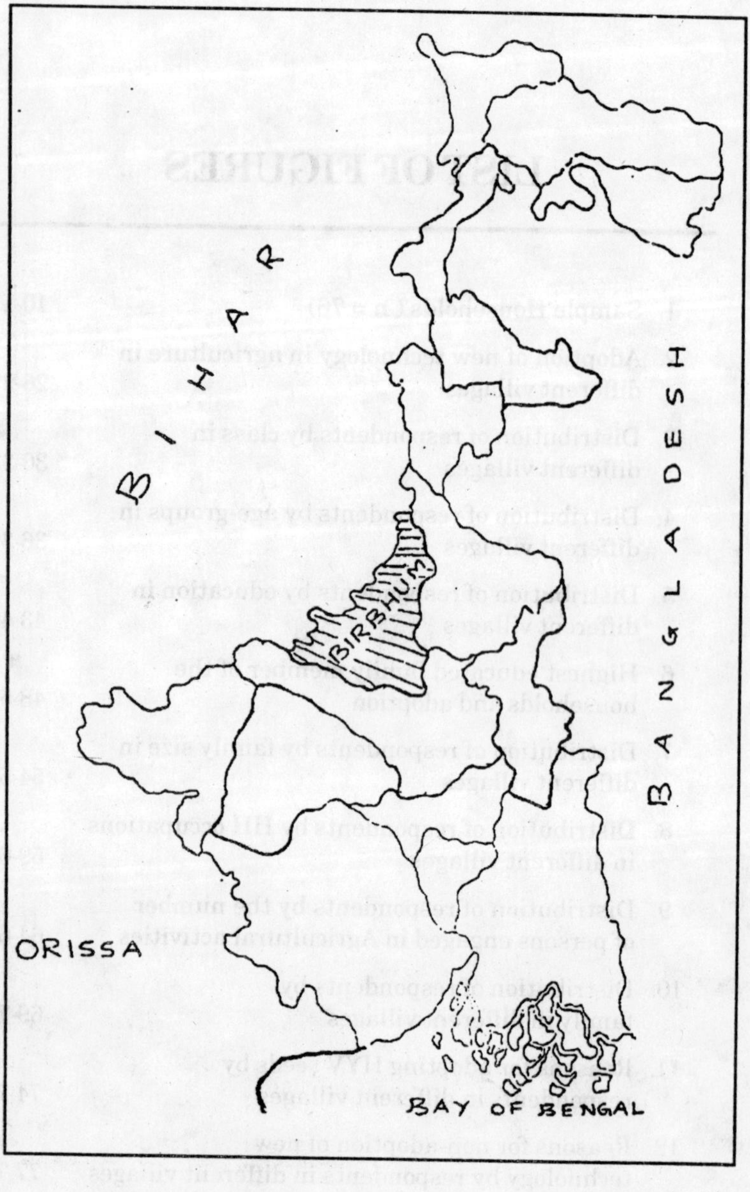

Map 1: Birbhum District (West Bengal)

Map 2: Location of Three Study villages : Kabilpur, Latapukur & Bamandiha

THE PROCESS

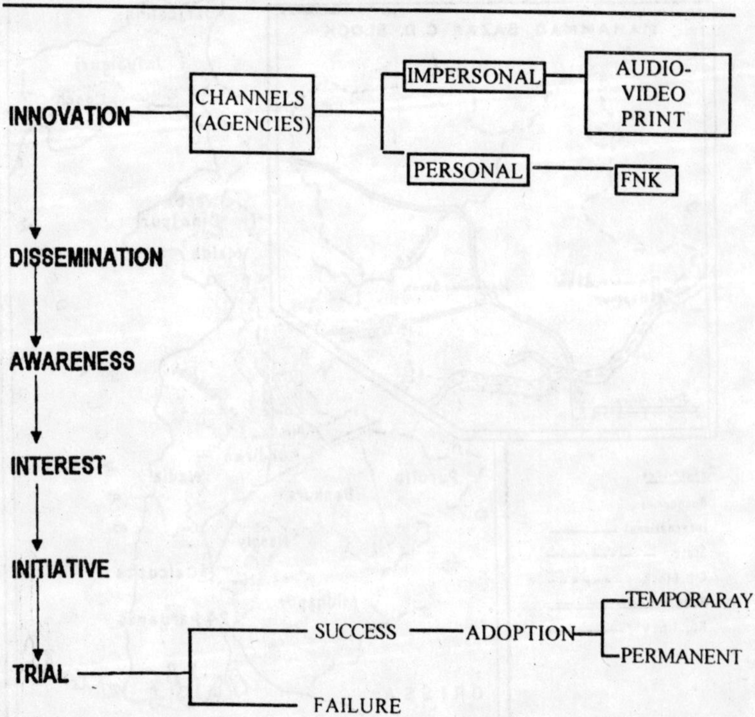
INNOVATION
CHANNELS (AGENCIES)
IMPERSONAL
AUDIO-VIDEO PRINT
PERSONAL
FNK
DISSEMINATION
AWARENESS
INTEREST
INITIATIVE
TRIAL
SUCCESS
ADOPTION
TEMPORARAY
PERMANENT
FAILURE

PROLOGUE

More than two decades ago (1980s), I had the opportunity of travelling through the villages of Md. Bazar Block in the district of Birbhum (West Bengal). Those trips were in connection with my profession as a Researcher in Sociological Research Unit of Indian Statistical Institute, Calcutta.

On my first visit I travelled by Gaya Passenger starting at 8.30 p.m. from Sealdah Railway Station and reached Sainthia early in the morning, next day. I had to wait for a local bus. That took me to the village, Patelnagar, 12 km away from Sainthia Railway Station. Patelnagar, was the locale of the block office. It took a little more than two hours by bus to cover 12 km. This bus was known as 'Murir tin' as the local bus passengers used to call it. The condition of the bus was very poor. Still, the bus was packed up for the frequency of the service was so less that every body tried to dash himself inside the bus desperately.

There was no metal road and the bus travelled through dusty 'bandh'. The path was full of ditches and potholes. That appeared to me as an endurance test. All the passengers had to bear with the jerks and there was horrible sound generated from the very old engine and dilapidated body of the bus. The road being very narrow, it was difficult to allow a 'pass' to the other vehicles coming from the opposite direction. The journey to

Patelnagar from Sainthia Railway Station appeared to be an ordeal.

I visited twenty-one villages in the Block and established rapport with the villagers and started collecting different information from the villagers.

Most of the villages had no approach road and it was difficult to enter the villages even on foot. All approach-roads were 'Kachha' and those too were full of wild bushes. It was more difficult to cross these roads during rainy season. The bus route was far away from the villages.

It should also be mentioned that, of these, some villages like Latapakur, Bamundiha (Tribal villages) were situated inside the jungles. The villagers were forced to come back to their villages before sunset after they worked outside the villages. There was no definite approach road to enter Latapakur, Bamundiha villages that were surrounded by jungles and hillocks and these were very remote from modern civilization. Though there were no ferocious wild animals, snakes and foxes in the jungles and hillocks would be abundant.

The villages were poor. Most of the villagers were labourers and they had no job in the villages. That is why they had to outmigrate to distant villages even to Dumka (Bihar) for job opportunities. For many months in a year they remained ill fed, ill-clothed and were in very ill-health. 'Tanr' land comprised a major portion of their land holdings. The soil was so hard that they could not cultivate those properly. There was no irrigation facility. All the agricultural fields were dry except in rainy seasons. The condition of the draft animals was also poor. Ponds were dry. No adequate drinking water facility was available. There was a lone tube-well at

Latapukur, which was even out of use. Cows and bullocks were reduced almost to skeletons and the conditions of the people were also very bad.

There is a village, Baidyanathpur, which is, situated 3 km away from these two villages. Baidyanathpur was more or less affluent village (Rajput dominated). Most of the villagers of Baidyanathpur were cultivators. The villagers of Latapakur and Bamundiha were employed as labourer, Mahindar of the landowners at Baidynathpur. These landowners would keep the labourers coming from Latapakur, Bamundiha and other villages tied to their land by 'Mahajani' loan. So they remained bonded to do work under those landlords at a very low wage. They, therefore, did not have enough scope to cultivate their own land if they had any.

The village, Kabilpur was a multiethnic village. The conditions of the villagers were not as bad as at Latapakur and Bamundiha. Even then, there were not enough jobs for most of the villagers for which they had to go to distant villages as well as in other districts even to other states in search of opportunities. Only a few of them would be able to come back at the time of plantation and harvesting. The land was used for one crop, namely aman paddy. There were no crops in winter season. Very few lands could be used for double cropping. There was little irrigation. All the ponds were dry in summer. Market was at a long distance (Sainthia).

In 1990s, I had to undertake further visits to some of these villages in connection with my Ph.D. work while I undertook a study on the leadership and development situations. But what attracted my attention most was that there had been remarkable and welcome changes in these villages during the decade. This was not only true for Kabilpur village but also for Latapukur and the neighbouring Bamundiha. Though the levels of changes in each of the villages were not same, there was marked prosperity everywhere. The approach roads to the villages became much better, and villagers were mainly engaged in their own agricultural field. Even in winter, there were a few patches of green in the fields, which could not even be thought of ten years ago.

I also noticed that villagers were changed in terms of their life styles and their attitudes towards agricultural practices also changed.

These changes after the interval of one decade attracted my interests. The process of change was not slow, rather quite fast. Now among the villagers there was a change in the perceptive levels about the modern technological amenities.

Naturally, I decided to enquire into the extent of such changes especially among the tribal peoples. Because, they are said to be untouched and unfocused, unexposed or little exposed to the outside world for the remoteness of their habitats as well as uniqueness of their style of living. It may also be mentioned that tribes in India did not attract proper attention either of the Government or of other Development Agencies until they became restive due to land and resource alienation in tribal areas (Kulkarni, S.D., 1975, Parulekar, G., 1975, Janardhan Rao, B., 1987).

This, in brief is the rationale of this study, which I undertook during the period between 1992 and 1994.

1

INTRODUCTION

The study is about Dissemination and Adoption of New Technologies in agricultural activities among the tribals. Agriculture in India forms the basic economic structure. Majority of our active population is engaged in cultivation and agriculture shapes the basis of the structural relationship of our society as a whole, i.e., the socio-political structure. If one flips through the pages of history, he can see this fact crystal-clear. At different points of time, movements and insurgencies of diverse nature have let the structure of agrarian society undergo changes. Side by side, various efforts for the advancement of our domestic economy have brought this aspect into focus.

The question of land reforms and mechnisation of land is now much stressed upon facts. To boost the agro-economy, to give a fillip to the psyche of agrarian populace and to eradicate the poverty at grass root level, the reformation of land and mechanization of cultivations are new much practiced and clamored phenomena in the current time. Scientists and technologists are endevouring for devices to banish the agricultural failures and the planners are active to pursue different models and methods that, to their belief, might bear fruits.

However, the farmers, who are said to be very much pre-occupied with their age-old practices and traditional notions, come into conflicts with the new idea envisaged and implemented by the agencies—institutional or non-institutional. Hence, there remains always a need to understand as well as to examine this particular area of human behaviour.

Different studies showed that among the total agricultural population, tribes hold a discernible proportion. Historically the tribals have been subjected to humiliation and oppression and have been deprived even of the minimum infrastructure of cultivation. Being evicted from the lands of their own and compelled to serve the others, the tribals have been lagging behind over the years. Still, the overall change in the agricultural scene and socio-political structure might have cast an influence over this downtrodden segment.

Now the question arises that how much benefit of growth and development have been percolated to the tribal, be it the question of land reforms or development in science and technology? To what extent this has been enjoyed by the traditionally downtrodden, unfocussed section known as tribals? What are the contradictions that have been generated out of this change and what is the process they fit themselves into the changing socio-polity?

The tribal agriculture was generally characterized as shifting cultivation- natural farming (Koraput in Orissa) and settled agriculture etc. in terms of "peasant mode of production". Whatever may be the nature of cultivation, it is generally held that the tribals are traditional in all their life-style and practices. Tribal Agriculture, therefore, also is not an exception.

But incidentally while evaluating a project run by HFCL, I observed some tribal habitats adopted modern technologies. This, it seemed to be intriguing as the tribal were supposed to be intriguing from mainstream and had very little access to power, education and 'contacts'.

Therefore, to understand the changes in the socio-political structure that have already occurred, there is a need to go through the dissemination and adoption process of the tribal about the new and modern technologies in agriculture.

By dissemination we would mean that the idea is transferred from one agency to outside the agency. The idea might have been generated through different scientific experimentations, say in laboratories or in fields. Now if the results of experimentations come to the benefit of others, that is to say, if the idea generated becomes beneficial to the target population, dissemination starts from the laboratories or the fields and serves as a pre-requisite to internalization of the idea by the said population. Without dissemination no idea can reach the people who might benefit out of that.

Now there comes the question of the channels of communication. Because if there is no communication, no dissemination can take place. There could be many channèls of communication. But for this particular study only those channels should be regarded which were used by the tribals in particular. Because, "channels of communication used by farmers influence their adoption behaviour, for communicators of information not only inform but also influence farmers regarding the adoption of improved farming practices[1]".

---

1. Satadal Dasgupta, *Diffusion of Agricultural Innovations in Village India*, p. 126, Wiley Eastern Limited, 1989.

These communication channels are classified broadly into institutional and non-institutional; personal and impersonal types. By institutional channels we mean, the channels that are developed for the specific purpose of disseminating information. That includes different Governmental and non-Governmental Agencies, like Statutory Agencies viz. Block, Panchayat, J.L.R.O., Agricultural Extension Office, Model farmers and non-statutory or Voluntary Agencies. Again there may be regular meeting places like market, Hat, Festival, and Fair etc., which are regarded as important non-institutional channels of communication to the farmers.

Impersonal channels do not involve any inter-personal contact between the communicator and recipient of information. Any kind of mass media namely, Radio, TV, Newspaper, Journals etc. fall in this category. But a point to note here is that the media engaged in audio or audio-visual (i.e., Radio and TV) information play much more important role than the media catering information in printed form to the recipients. Because, the print media have less access to the farmers, tribals in particular, as the level of education and literacy is low among them. The rural populaces have little access to education and as they are mostly illiterate, Radio and TV are regarded as major impersonal channels of information.

Personal channels involve interface between two or more individuals exchanging information. This includes friends, neighbours and kins, the other farmers as well as the extension agents.

Hence, any idea can be disseminated to the cultivators if they are exposed to any one of the channels of communication.

After dissemination of the idea or ideas, there comes the question of adoption.

By adoption we would mean, a decision to carry out the ideas or innovations by an individual or a group of individuals, the decision to adopt an idea, however, "is not normally a single, instantaneous act[1]". It involves a process, which is called the adoption process. This process involves a period of time during which an adopter goes through a number of stages, be it physical or mental before making a final decision to adopt an idea[2]. The stages comprise awareness, interest, evaluation, trial and then adoption.

For the awareness, exposition of an individual adopter or a group of adopters of the disseminated information is of prime importance. Naturally, for this exposition to information the infrastructure around the adopter or a group of adopter plays a pivotal role. If the individual adopter or the group of adopters enjoy an improved infrastructure amenities, he or that group is much more exposed to the information and hence is/are supposed to be quick adopter.

Now if one is exposed to information, 'interest' starts playing its role. At this stage, the individual/group develops enough interest about a disseminated idea to seek more information and knowledge about it in terms of its nature, function, modus operandi and utility.

Hence, if he crosses the stage of 'interest', he then starts evaluating the idea. This is called the evaluation stage. The adopter(s) then evaluate(s) the usefulness and relative benefit of the idea in relation to available

---

1. Jones, The adoption and diffusion of agricultural practices, *World Agricultural Economics and Rural Sociology Abstract*, 9: P 1-34, 1967.
2. S. Dasgupta - *op. cit.*, p.43.

alternatives. Basically, the adopters attempt to visualize the expected outcome if they adopt the idea. Naturally, here occurs a question of conviction. If the adopter or adopters are convinced enough about the disseminated ideas, if those ideas happen to be more tangible, then the adopter or adopters opt for the 'trial'.

By 'trial' we mean, the trying out of an idea on a small scale, which provides the individual adopter with the opportunity to evaluate the applicability of the idea to his personal situation in more concrete and tangible terms. If the trials fail, the idea would not be accepted by the individual farmer(s). Otherwise, the farmer(s) would internalize the idea into his or their system of farming operation. Then, and only then, it can be said, that the disseminated idea has been adopted.

Now, as we are concerned about the adoption of new technologies, we should define what we would mean by new technologies. By new technologies, we would mean, not only the developed implements and the accessories that have been introduced or to be introduced in the agricultural arena but also inputs like improved or HYV seeds, chemical fertilizer etc. and the scientific research or the technological aspect of agriculture that has brought about a new breed of high yielding seeds, fertilizers, crop conservative pesticides which have enabled the agricultural practices to be more technology oriented instead of the traditional practices of the farmers, tribal in particular. These new techno-logies includes, use of improved (HYV) seed, chemical fertilizers, tractor, irrigation, power tiller, and modern practices like line sowing, wet seedbed, three ploughing, distance of heels, plants per heel etc..

OBJECTIVES

The objective of the study was first to understand the extent of dissemination of new technologies in agriculture among the tribes. For this, one has to have information about the following:

(i) What did the farmers practice during 1980-81 and 1993.

(ii) What they are practicing in 1992-93.

(iii) What are 'new' in the current practices compared to the older ones?

(iv) Where from they got these ideas and how they thought of adopting these.

Secondly, the study sought to identify the factors contributing to the replacement of traditional system of agriculture among the tribals.

The questions to be answered for tackling this issue would be

(i) Why are the farmers interested to adopt new technologies?

(ii) Whether increase in family size of these tribal households motivated the farmers in technological adoption?

(iii) Are the technologies now more accessible than in previous years?

(iv) Do they get the new implements or packages at subsidized rate?

Through this study we would try to suggest what should be the proper method of extension of technology for the tribals.

To do this we have to know the technologies or the packages that were already present in their agricultural system. Again, we also have to understand the policy prescriptions advocated by the agronomists, Governmental Agency or Voluntary Agencies to them and whether they could internalize those prescriptions. If they did not, then why? What were the constraints for adopting those prescriptions?

AREA OF THE STUDY

I worked in three villages, Kabilpur was a multiethnic village, and Latapakur and Bamundiha were two tribal villages. I included only Tribal (Santhal) population of Kabilpur in order to study only the tribal farmers, Latapukur and Bamundiha are mono ethnic, (Santhals). These three villages are situated in Md. Bazar block and in two Gram Panchayats. Kabilpur village is situated in Angargaria Gram Panchayat, whereas Latapakur and Bamundiha two adjacent villages are situated in Charicha Gram Panchayat. Charicha Gram Panchayat is situated in the border of Bihar and West Bengal.

Sample

In order to study the adoption of new technology in agriculture among tribals, the study focused on those tribal farmers, who owned and had command over land. Hence in each of the three villages, I had to identify the land operators, as they were supposed to be the decision makers in case of adopting any new idea.

For this, I excluded the households which might be owning land but do not operate. There are such cases at Kabilpur and Latapakur.

At Kabilpur, there are six such cases out of which five are labourers who do not cultivate their land uneconomic being the holdings. Another persons is engaged in trade, possessing a little of inferior-quality land. He also does not cultivate the land.

At Latapakur, there are twelve cases out of which ten are labourers. They do not cultivate their land. Because they have very little land which is again uncultivated fallow. Another two persons leased out their land to other cultivators because they are physically handicapped.

At Kabilpur, therefore, only 31 out of 78 tribal households were chosen who owned and operated land. At Latapakur and Bamundiha 33 and 12 such households were chosen out of the totals of 64 and 14 respectively. Hence, a total of 76 out of 156 households came under this study.

Table - 1 : Sample Households (n=76*)

Village	Tribal Hhs	Land-less	Land owners	Non operators	Opera-ting Hhs
(1)	(2)	(3)	(4)	(5)	(6)
Kabilpur	78	41	37	6	31
Latapakur	64	19	45	12	33
Bamundiha	14	2	12	0	12
Total	156	62	94	18	76

Source: Survey 1992-93.

NATURE AND METHODS OF DATA COLLECTION

Nature of information :

The information were collected on different aspects of demography, education (literacy), occupational, natural

Figure 1: Sample Household (n=76)

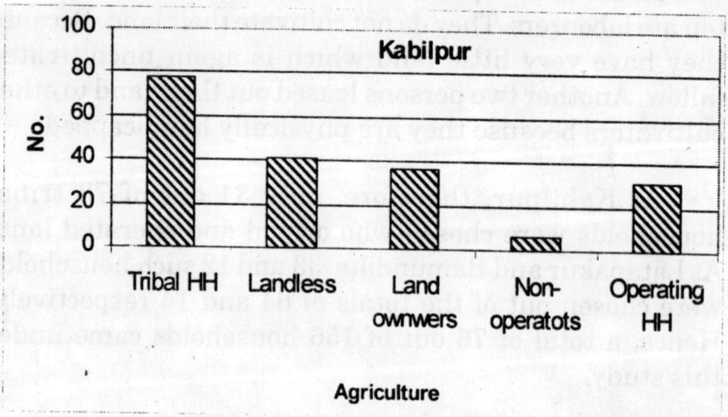

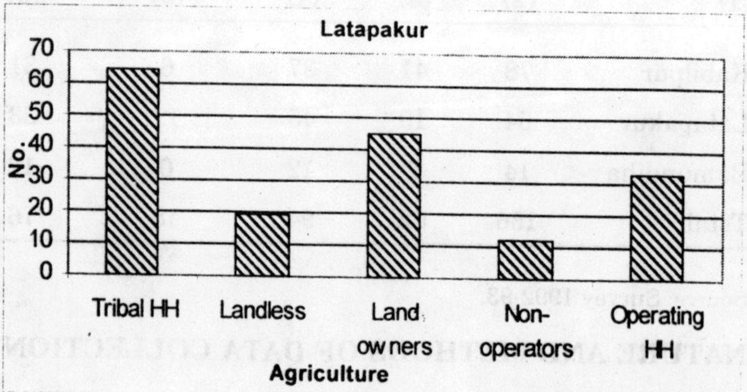

Fig. 1 : contd.

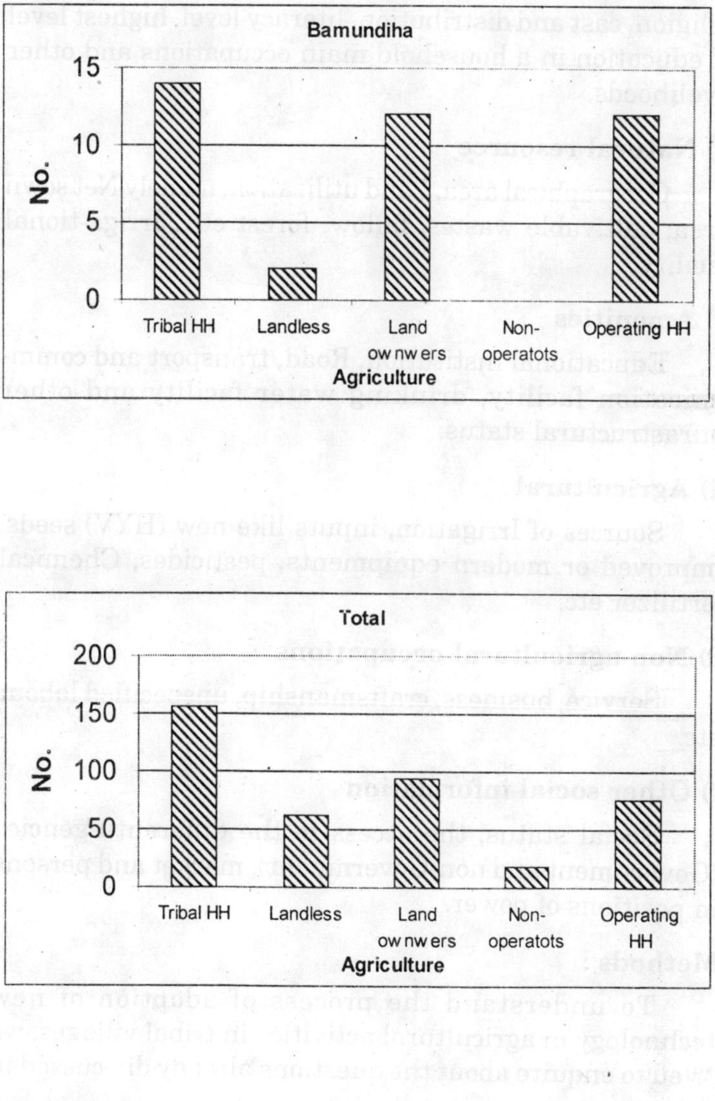
Bamundiha
15
10
5
0
No.
Tribal HH
Landless
Land ow nw ers
Non- operatots
Operating HH
Agriculture
Total
200
150
100
50
0
No.
Tribal HH
Landless
Land ow nw ers
Non- operatots
Operating HH
Agriculture

resources, amenities, agricultural systems, and various other social and cultural state of affairs.

a) Demographic

Data on household - compositions, population, sex, religion, cast and distribution, literacy level, highest level of education in a household main occupations and other livelihoods.

b) Natural resource

Geographical area, Land utilization, namely Net sown area, cultivable wastes, fallow, forest etc., Irriga-tional facility.

c) Amenities

Educational institution, Road, transport and comm-unication facility, drinking water facility and other infrastructural status.

d) Agricultural

Sources of Irrigation, inputs like new (HYV) seeds, improved or modern equipments, pesticides, Chemical fertilizer etc.

e) Non-agricultural occupations

Service, business, craftsmanship, unspecified labour etc.

f) Other social information

Social status, the access to the different agencies (Government and non-Government), market and persons in positions of power.

Methods :

To understand the process of adoption of new technology in agricultural activities in tribal villages, we tried to enquire about the questions already dis-cussed in previous section (objectives). We canvassed pre ordained and pre-tested questionnaire among the respondents. Besides, we conducted unrestrained dialogues, which were noted, in our diaries. We used to put down all other information in a notebook and check the consistency of notes in subsequent meetings with the respondents. Initially we had a checklist as to what information we intended to have to understand the process of dissemination and adoption and also the people who were adopting those. In the second stage a moderately long and pre-ordained schedule in regional language was pre-tested and recast according to the need. Besides collecting the materials, on the basis of structured schedules and questionnaire, we conducted open-ended interviews. I spent times in the houses of respondents, 'Chanditalas', clubs, schools, agricultural fields, and shops of various villages. Most of the time I remained a listener and sought occasional explanations or clarifications when needed.

The village level information was collected through unrestrained and tireless dialogue with the knowledgeable villagers. Checking and cross checking of information was done by interrogating a few practicing farmers. After completion of fieldwork, the original information were transcribed and tabulated using standard sociological and anthropological techniques.

To analyse and to infer anything about the proposed research queries we primarily based on the survey data.

Again we had to collect secondary information from Block Office, Agricultural Extention Office, Settlement Office, Panchayats etc.

Besides using descriptive-analytical method Multivariate Analysis has been done to understand the most significant factors contributing to the extent of adoption.

LIMITATION OF THE STUDY

As mentioned earlier the study has certain limitations. It is a study of exploratory nature. Naturally, further similar studies are called for in different agro-climatic zones to formulate comprehensive database. There are other limitations also in this study, which are the following :

1. We could not take into account any non-tribal group for comparison with tribals.
2. More villages under different ecological zones should have featured in this study.
3. Scarcity of time and resources also hindered the scope of this study.
4. We could not make in-depth study onto whether all the new accessories and implements were subsidized by the government.
5. What were the exact prescriptions advocated by the agronomists and other developing agencies was not studied thoroughly and categorically. It was simply considered that the packages amenable to change in the agricultural scene of area under study were disseminated some how, by some agencies and adopted by the tribals. That is why partial adoption and the reasons for those were not quite apparent.

2

REVIEW OF RELATED LITERATURE

The present researcher, a student of sociology thought worthwhile to make a very brief review of the tradition of research on dissemination and adoption process. The major researches were done by sociologists, anthropologists, educationists, market researchers, economists and others including mass communicators. Every behavioural science and recently agricultural science show interest in the dissemination and adoption process of new ideas. Studies on agricultural technology disse-mination and adoption process specially farmer's decision about adoption of new technology attracted the attention of a number of scholars as to how a farmer is influenced while making a decision regarding adoption of new farm practices even when he is within the existing farming system.

Some diffusionists aim to retrace the whole complex dispersion of human culture and to discover origins, believed to be few. Father Wilhelm Schmidt, foremost protagonist of the *Kulturhistorische method*, arrested that the specific task of ethnology is '.... Not only to understand the conditions existing among the primitive people today, but also to recognize in them witnesses and survivals of the oldest development of mankind...' and with their help to construct the objective succession of events and thereby the actual genesis of culture among the different people (W. Schmidt, 1939).

According to Rogers (1962), diffusion is the process, which an innovation spreads. The diffusion process is the spread of a new idea from its source of invention or creation to its ultimate users or adopters.

Every behavioral science and recently agricultural science have interest in the diffusion of new ideas. Studies on agricultural technology diffusion specially farmer's decision about adoption of new technology attracted the attention of a number of scholars as to how a farmer is influenced while making a decision regarding adoption of new farm practices even when he is within the existing farming system.

Farmer's decision are greatly influenced by attitude and relationships within the local communities in which they live (Mosher, 1966). Individual's activities, whatever and whenever it may be, are influenced largely by the situation, in which an individual lives and works. A good deal of variation in behaviour is a result of variation in the immediate situation, the individual finds himself at different times (Murthy, 1969). It is for this reason that the environment in which a farmer lives has to be studied to make out 'what causes what'. The situational aspect influencing the adoption behaviour of farmers can be viewed from different angles, one of which being the distance of habitance of farmers from village to village, hamlet to hamlet, etc. The village or hamlet in our society, no matter how small, is still subjected to countless urban influences. The rural-urban differential is therefore a gradient, with the rural end of the scale never even approaching absolute rurality (Davis, 1940). This view has been amply shared by many scientists (Redfield, 1947; Dexter, 1964; Anderson and Ishwaran, 1965).

In Redfield's (1947) model of folk-urban continuum the people at the urban pole would be higher in edu-cation, general knowledge and contact with extension-agents. Various other workers reported association of urbanization with literacy, participation in formal social organization, socio-economic status, risk proneness, adoptiveness and so on (Lerner, 1958; Bose, 1961; Anderson and Ishwaran, 1965; Schramm and Ruggles, 1967). Urbanization was found to be influencing farmer's adoptiveness (Acharya, 1956; Rao, 1958; Gist and Fays, 1965; Ray, 1975).

Ross (1958) has made diffusion research findings in agriculture by Lionberger (1960) and in education. The education was not found to be independent of urban influence. The difference between the two groups with regard to the farmers' educational attainment seems to have been resulted not only due to lack of adequate faci-lities for acquisition of formal education in low urba-nized villages but also due to inaccessibility of those villages creating barriers to the residents of low urba-nized villages in sending their children elsewhere for attending the schools.

Katz (1961) and Katz and Levin (1959) studied diffusion as those tracing the elements of (1) a given new idea, (2) overtime (3) through specific channels of communication, and (4) within a social structure.

Kroeber (1923) and Wissler (1923) traced the diffusion of horse from the Spanish explorers to American Indian tribes and their findings were how idea differs from one society to another. Linton (1952) held the characteristics of an innovation affect its rate of adoption and Sharp (1952) studied the effects of the adoption of the steel axe by an

Australian native tribe. Their findings indicated that diffusion is the consequ-ence of innovations.

Pembertion (1936) and Bowers (1938) investigated rural-urban differences in the rate of adoption of radios. Wilson and his associate Gallup (1955) had studied the ratio of innovations to the relative cost of their diffu-sion. Barton (1961) studied the diffusion of educational methods for teaching retarded children among school systems. Their findings were correlates of innovative-ness.

Trade (1903) suggested that the adoption of new ideas followed a normal, S-shaped distribution over time. At first, only a few individuals adopt the new idea, then great number of individuals accept the innovation, and finally the rate of adoption slackens. His findings were S-shaped adopter distribution. Chapin (1928) studied the diffusion of the city manager plan of government. He also followed Trade's lead in showing that the adapter distribution for the City Manager idea in the United States followed an S-shaped 'growth curve'.

Kollmorgen (1941), Hoffer (1942) studied the adoption of farm ideas by German Swiss farmers and non-German Swiss farmers. Their findings were charac-teristic of ideas related to their rate of adoption. Ryan and Gross (1943) studied the diffusion of hybrid seed crop in Iowa. Their findings were also the same as of Kollmorgen and Hoffer.

Polson and Pal (1955) in the Philippines, Wilkening (1962) and Wilkening and others (1960) in Australia and Lindstrom (1958) in Japan studied diffusion. Allen (1956) compared the diffusion of driver training; an innovation promoted by safety groups and car dealers, among pupils studying in the community. Mort and Cornell (1941), Coeking (1941), Barrington (1953), Lovos (1955), Adler (1955) and Allen (1956) studied the pattern of adoption of an educational idea over time. The findings of Polson and Pal, Allen et al, was S-shaped adopter distribution.

Caplow (1952) and Caplow and Raymond (1954) studied the diffusion of a medical drug. They sought mainly to determine the degree of influence of opinion leaders in the diffusion of drug among medical doctors. Their results showed that the opinion leaders had great degree of influence in the process of diffusion.

Armstrong (1959), in an ingenious analysis of secondary data, determined the relationship between types of promotional activities by change agents and resulting changes in the adoption of innovations by their clients. He found that for the Kentucky countries he analyzed, greater the promotions efforts by country extension agents, the greater the adoption of innovations by farmers in their countries.

Dissemination of information on agricultural innovations must preceed their adoption by individual farmers. There is a close relationship between the channels of communication used by farmers and their adoption behaviour, for communicators of information also influence the decision of farmers regarding the adoption of agricultural innovations. The role of communication channels in the adoption and diffusion of agricultural innovations have great importance.

Pachori, R.S. and Tripathi, S.G. (1983)'s study conducted in Madhya Pradesh showed that 100 percent of the farmers mentioned friends, neighbours, and relatives as source of information for diffusion of agricultural activities. 'Other farmers' were also the most frequently sought sources of information in a Maharashtra village (Supe, 1971). Supe found in his study, a statistically significant positive correlation between the use of the print mass media and adoption behaviours.

Low literacy rate and poor accessibility to the mass media appear to be the two most important contributing factors to the negligible use of both print and non-print mass media by farmers. The impersonal quality of the mass media is also a determining factor of its low credibility and use. The face-to-face exchange between the communicator and the recipient of information is an important element in decision making, especially in traditional societies (Patel and Pandey, 1973).

Fliegel, Frederick (1967)'s study conducted in Uttar Pradesh showed that while the proportion of the non-literate farmers obtaining information from the print media was much smaller then the literate farmers, almost an identical proportions of the non-literate and literate farmers with equal access to radio listened to farm radio programmes and effectively obtained information from them. He concluded that exposure to agricultural information through the non-print media, such as radio and movies, is not significantly affected by the lack of ability to read and write as long as there is access to these sources.

A study in Bihar conducted by Singh, Singh and Mishra (1971) showed that small farmers obtained information on insecticides and Dwarf wheat from friends, neighbours, and relatives while farmers opera-ting large sized holdings relied on the mass media and institutional personal sources.

According to Mathur, Singh and Lokharde (1974), while the use of the mass media was insignificant by the farmers of all socioeconomic categories those of the higher status categories used institutional personal sources more frequently than the farmers belonging to the lower status categories.

The diffusion of an innovation within a social system takes place through its adoption by individuals of groups. 'Adoption' may be defined as the continued use by individuals or groups, of a recommended idea or practice over a reasonably long period of time. Adoption, however, is not a permanent behaviour. An individual may decide to discontinue the use of an innovation for a variety of personal, situational, or social reasons. An individual may also decide to reject an innovation after hearing about it even after trying it out on a small scale. 'If he thinks that' it will not serve his purpose or will not suit his personal, social or situational circumstances, he would discontinue adopting it.

Reddy and Murthy (1973) classified adoption in their study in Andhra Pradesh. After assigning an adoption score to each farmer according to the number of practices adopted, the means of the adoption scores of all farmers were calculated. The farmers whose adoption scores were above the mean plus one standard deviation (x + I s.d.) are categorized as 'high adopters', whose score were below the mean minus one standard deviation (x - I s.d.) are categorized as 'low adopters' and those whose scores were in between x + I s.d. and x - I s.d., are classified as 'medium adopters'.

'Relative advantages' as a characteristic of an adoption is not very different from what was described (Bose and Dasgupta, 1962) as utility. The relative advan-tages of an adoption are sometimes measured by its 'economic profitability' (Arul and Knight, 1977; Sahi and Pawar, 1966; Singh and Singh, 1980; Singh and Babu, 1988).

The advantage of an adoption is not always perceived in economic terms by its potential adopters. The farmers of western Uttar Pradesh villages rejected a high yielding variety of wheat because it was perceived to be socially disadvantageous (Supe, 1958).

The 'physical' and 'cultural' compatibility of an adoption is perceived in terms of its consistency with existing values and practices (Mular and Roy, 1965; Singh and Singh, 1980).

The relative simplicity of plant protection chemicals in terms of their use and application enabled them to be diffused rapidly in the villages of Barasat region in West Bengal (Bose, Dasgupta and Das, 1962).

For adopting new technology, Farmer's decision is greatly influenced by attitude and relationships within the local communities in which they live (Mosher, 1966). Individual's activities, whatever and whenever it may be, are influenced largely by the situation, in which the individual lives and works. A good deal of variation in behaviour is a result of variation in the immediate situation, the individual finds himself at different times (Reddy and Murthy; 1973). It is for this reason that the environment in which a farmer lives has to be studied to make out 'what causes what'. The situational aspect influencing the adoption behaviour of farmers can be viewed from different angles, one of which being the distance of habitats of farmers from village to village, hamlet-to-hamlet etc. The village or hamlet in our society, no matter how small, is still subjected to count-less urban influences. The rural - urban differential is therefore a gradient with the rural end of the scale never even approaching absolute rurality (Davis, 1966). This view has been amply shared by many scientists (Redfield, 1947; Dexter, 1964; Anderson and Ishwaran, 1965).

Urbanization was found to be influencing farmer's adoptiveness (Acharya, 1965; Rao, 1958; Gist and Faya, 1965; Pemberton, 1936 and Bowers, 1938) and rural - urban differences in the rate of adoption of radio. Their finding was correlates of innovativeness.

Similarly, Wilson and his associate Gallup (1955) were studying the ratio of innovations to the relative cost of their diffusion. Finding was correlates of innovativeness.

Mort and Cornell (1941), Coeking (1951), Barrington (1953), Lovos (1955), Adler (1955) and Allen (1956) studied the pattern of adoption of an educational idea over time. Their findings were S-shaped adopter distribution.

Paging through the various researches on the subject I became interested and also found that I was not new in this field. Previous researchers built up different concepts and theories on this area of research and I could test those with the empirical observations made in my study villages. But after compilation of the information I could have, I found the date need be treated in a little different manner. The reason for this was that the adoption process could not be properly understood without making a causal analysis. With resource and time constraints of an individual researcher, I also felt that my date suffer from several limitations which I would deal with in latter pages. While I greatly owe many ideas to my predecessors, I decided to add a few specific points revealed from the micro realities.

3

PROCESS OF DISSEMINATION AND ADOPTION

As mentioned in the previous section, our respondent households were 76 who owned and/or operated cultivable land and were in a position to undertake agronomic decisions. The persons who were not able to take any decision who were either land-less or non-operators were excluded from the discussion. The discussion therefore includes 76 land-operators who are all tribals and are spread in three study-villages.

Adopter and Non-adopter

Out of 76 respondents 65 (85.55%) adopted new technology and 11 (14.45%) did not.

If one considers the adoption-rate, the village, Kabilpur tops the list (90.23%), Latapakur comes second (84.85%) and Bamundiha figures third (75.00%), overall rate of adoption being (85.55%).

It reveals that the rate of adoption is quite high in all the three villages indicating that they are all keen about increasing their production (vide Table & figure 2).

Table 2 : Adoption of New Technology in agriculture in different villages (n=76)

Village Adoption	Kabilpur (%)	Latapakur (%)	Bamundiha (%)	Total
(1)	(2)	(3)	(4)	(5)
Non-Adopter	3 (9.68)	5 (15.15)	3 (25.00)	11 (14.45)
Adopter	28 (90.32)	28 (84.85)	9 (75.00)	55 (85.55)
Total	31(100.00)	33 (100.00)	12 (100.00)	76 (100.00)
	(49.79)	(43.92)	(15.79)	(100.00)

Source : Ibid.

Figure 2 : Adoption of New Technology in agriculture in different villages (n=76)

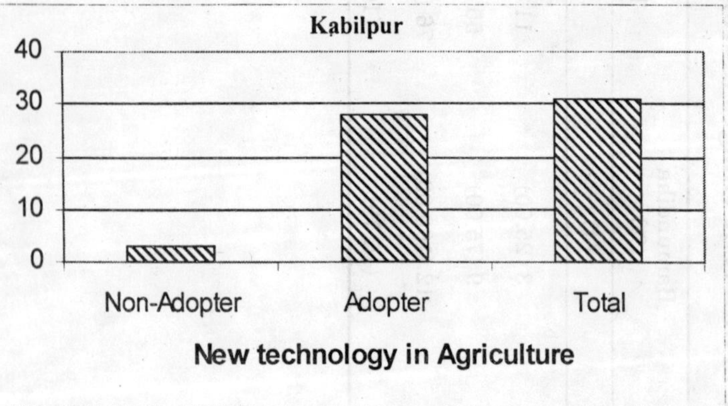

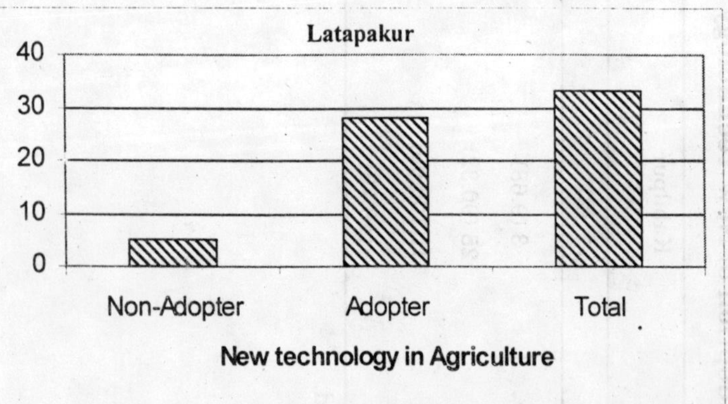

Figure 2 : Contd.

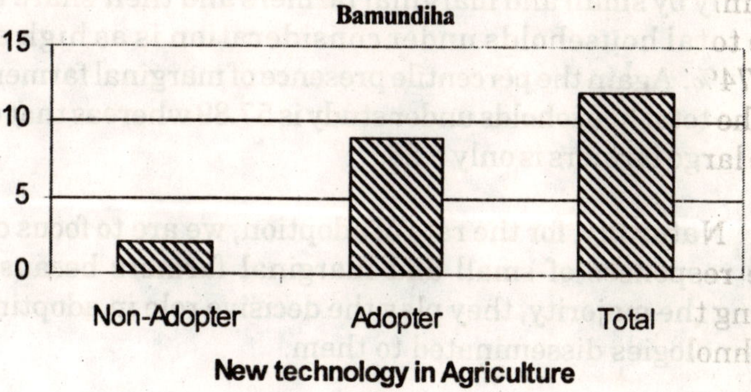

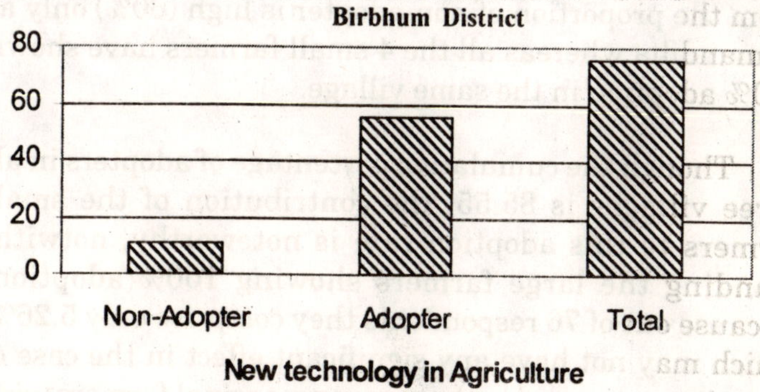

Adoption by farm size categories

The large farmers having operable land more than 15 bighas[1] are found at Kabilpur only and all of them adopted new technologies. But the other two villages are inhabited mainly by small and marginal farmers and their share in the total households under consideration is as high as 94.74%. Again the percentile presence of marginal farmers in the total households under study is 57.89 whereas that of the large farmers is only 5.26.

Naturally, for the rate of adoption, we are to focus on the responses of small and marginal farmers because, being the majority, they play the decisive role in adopting technologies disseminated to them.

It is notably observed that the small farmers of the three villages are well ahead in adoption as in Kabilpur and Bamandiha. They are 100% adopters and in Latapakur only one out of 11 was the odd man (!). Almost all the non-adopters in all three villages are marginal farmers owning less than 7.5 bighas of land. Out of total 11 non-adopters 10 are in this marginal group! And again among them the proportion of non-adopter is high (60%) only at Bamandiha whereas all the 4 small farmers have shown 100% adoption in the same village.

Though the cumulative percentage of adopters in all three villages is 85.55, the contribution of the small farmers to this adoption rate is noteworthy, notwithstanding the large farmers showing 100% adoption. Because out of 76 respondents they comprise only 5.26% which may not have any significant effect in the case of adoption, compared to that among marginal farmers (vide Table and Figure 3).

---

1. One Bigha (local measure) amounts to 0.33 acre.

Table 3: Distribution of respondents by Class in different villages

Village → Class	Kabilpur			Latapakur			Bamundiha			Grand Total		
	A*	NA**	Total	A	NA	Total	A	NA	Total	A	NA	Total
(1)	(2)	(3)	(4)	(5)	(6)	(7)	(8)	(9)	(10)	(11)	(12)	(13)
Large (>15 bigha)	4 (100.00)	0 (0.00)	4 (100.00)	0	0	0	0	0	0	4 (100.00)	0 (0.00)	4 (5.26) (100.00)
Small (>7.5 bigha <15 bigha)	13 (100.00)	0 (0.00)	13 (100.00)	10	1	11	4	0	4	27 (96.43)	1 (3.57)	28 (36.85) (100.00)
Marginal (≤7.5bigha)	11 (78.57)	3 (21.43)	14 (100.00)	18	4	22	5	3	8	34 (77.27)	10 (22.73)	44 (57.89) (100.00)
Total	28 (90.32)	3 (9.68)	31 (100.00)	28	5	33	9	3	12	65 (85.55)	11 (14.45)	76 (100.00) (100.00)

*A = Adopter; **NA = Non-Adopter,
Source: Ibid.

Figure 3: Distribution of Respondents by Class in Different Villages

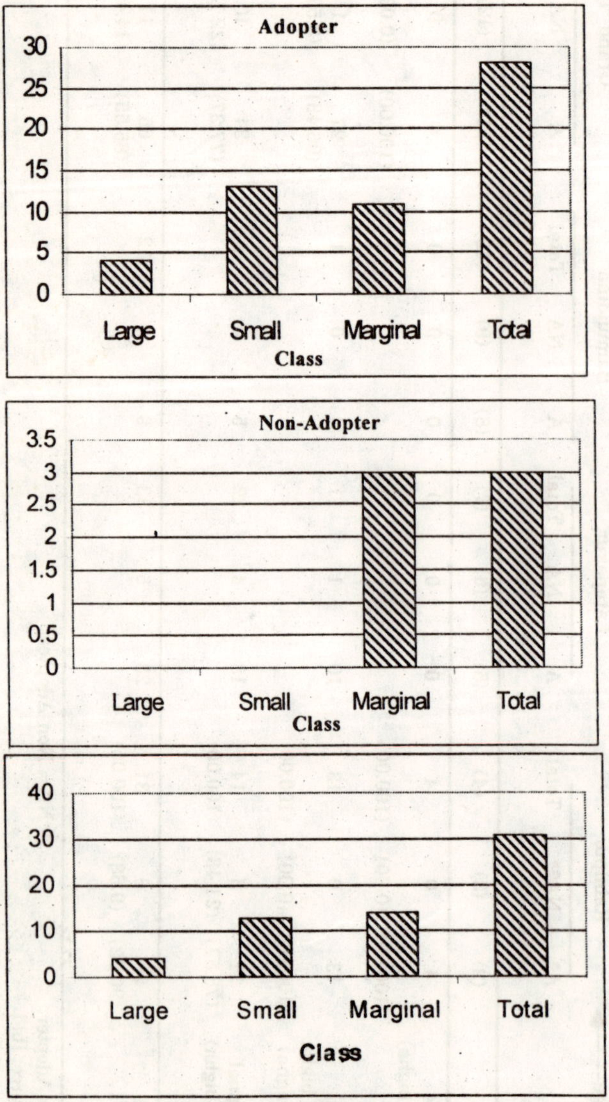

Kabilpur

Figure 3: Contd.

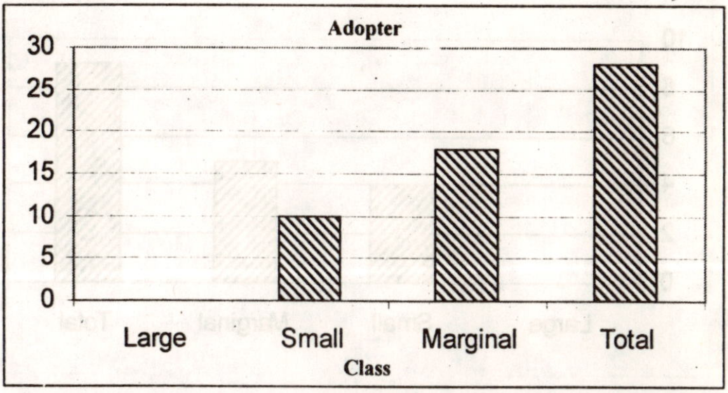

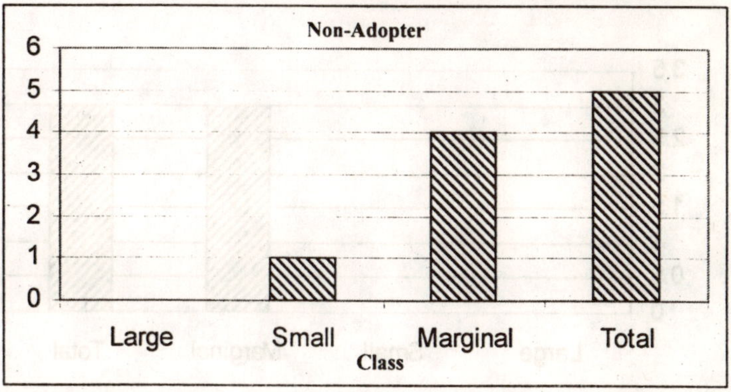

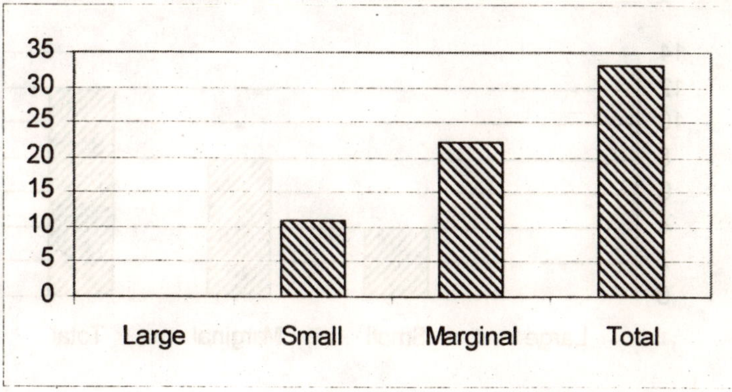

Latapakur

Figure 3: Contd.

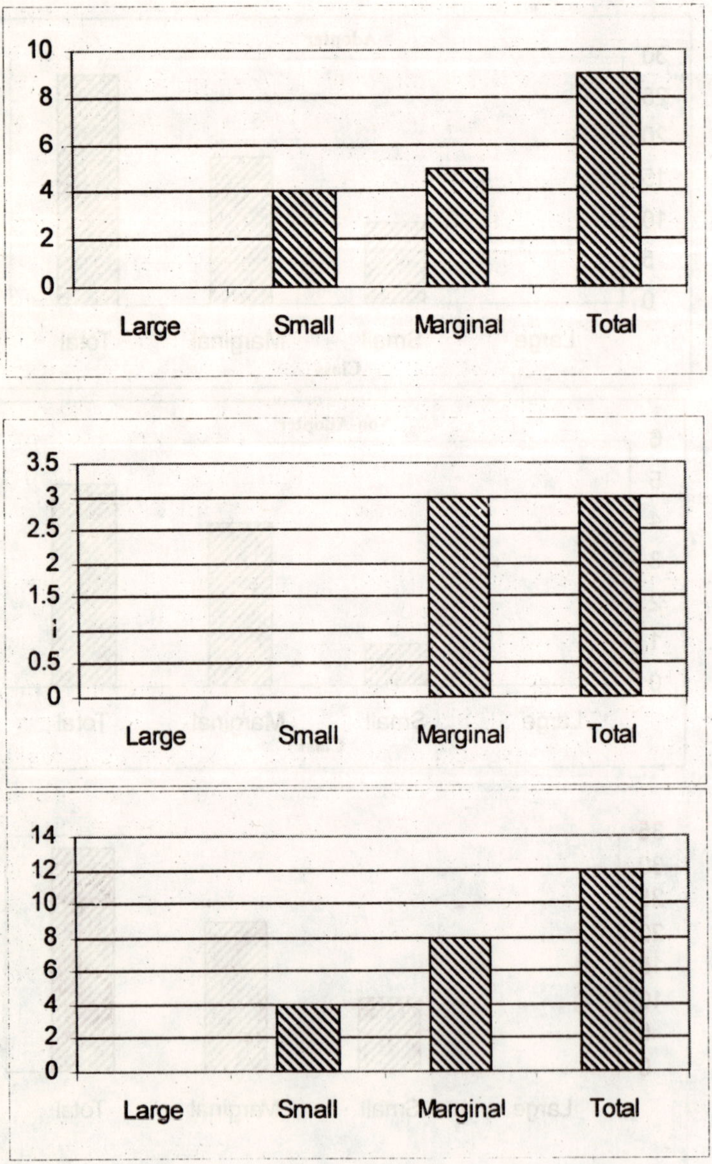

Bamundiha

Figure 3: Contd.

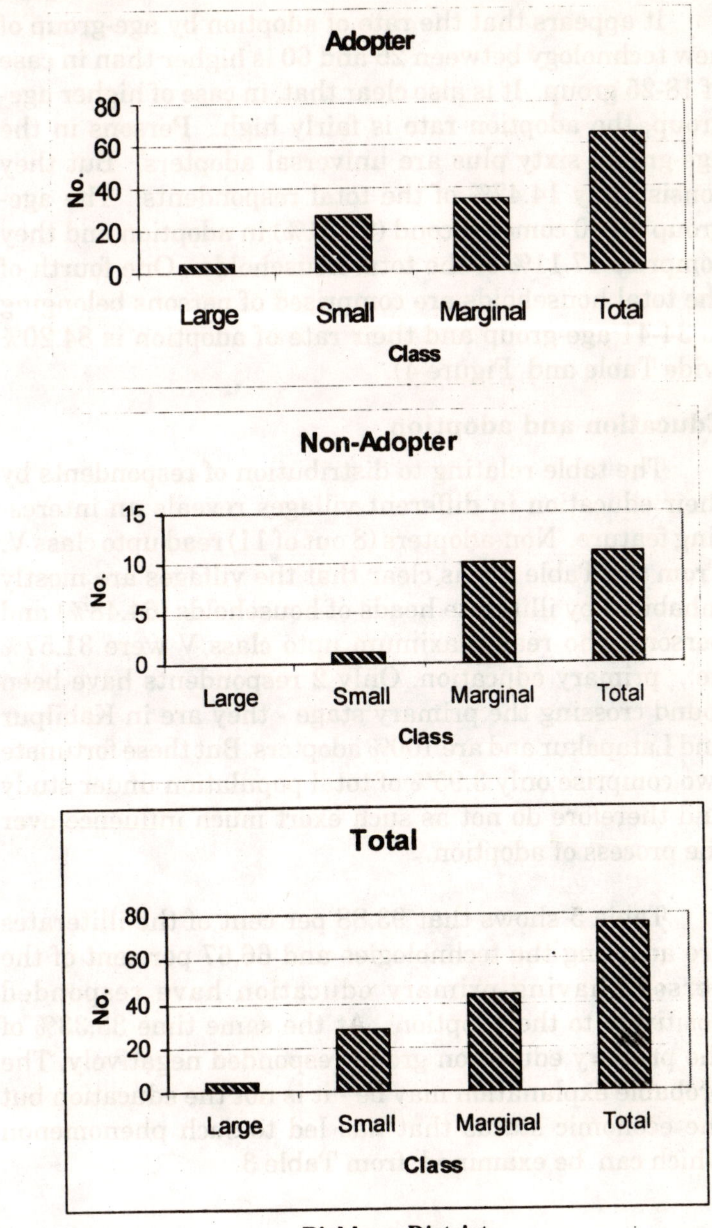

Birbhum District

Adoption by age groups

It appears that the rate of adoption by age-group of new technology between 26 and 60 is higher than in case of 18-25 group. It is also clear that, in case of higher age-group, the adoption rate is fairly high. Persons in the age-group, sixty plus are universal adopters. But they consist only 14.47% of the total respondents. The age-group 50-60 comes second (92.31%) in adoption and they comprise 17.11% of the total households. One fourth of the total households are comprised of persons belonging to 34-41 age-group and their rate of adoption is 84.20% (vide Table and Figure 4).

Education and adoption

The table relating to distribution of respondents by their education in different villages reveals an interesting feature. Non-adopters (8 out of 11) read upto class V. From the Table 5 it is clear that the villages are mostly inhabited by illiterate heads of households (64.48%) and persons who read maximum upto class V were 31.57% i.e., primary education. Only 2 respondents have been found crossing the primary stage - they are in Kabilpur and Latapakur and are 100% adopters. But these fortunate two comprise only 3.95% of total population under study and therefore do not as such exert much influence over the process of adoption.

Table 5 shows that 93.88 per cent of the illiterates are adopting the technologies and 66.67 per cent of the persons having primary education have responded positively to the adoption. At the same time 33.33% of the primary education group responded negatively. The probable explanation may be - it is not the education but the economic status that has led to such phenomenon which can be examined, from Table 3.

Table 4: Distribution of respondents by age-groups in different villages

Village→	Kabilpur			Latapakur			Bamundiha			Grand Total		
Age group	A*	NA**	Total	A	NA	Total	A	NA	Total	A	NA	Total
(1)	(2)	(3)	(4)	(5)	(6)	(7)	(8)	(9)	(10)	(11)	(12)	(13)
18-25	2	1	3	-	1	1	-	1	1	2 (40.00)	3 (60.00)	5 (6.58) (100.00)
26-33	9	-	9	2	2	4	3	-	3	14 (87.50)	2 (12.50)	16(21.05) (100.00)
34-41	7	-	7	8	1	9	1	2	3	16 (84.20)	3 (13.30)	19(25.00) (100.00)
42-49	4	2	6	5	-	5	1	-	1	10 (83.33)	2 (16.67)	12(15.79) (100.00)
50-60	4	-	4	6	1	7	2	-	2	12 (92.31)	1 (7.69)	13(17.11) (100.00)
60+	2	-	2	7	-	7	2	-	2	11 (100.00)	0 (0.00)	11 (14.47) (100.00)
Total	28	3	31	28	5	33	9	3	12	65 (85.55)	11 (14.45)	76(100.00) (100.00)

* A = Adopter
** NA = Non-adopter Source : Ibid

Figure 4: Distribution of Respondents by Age-group in Different Villages

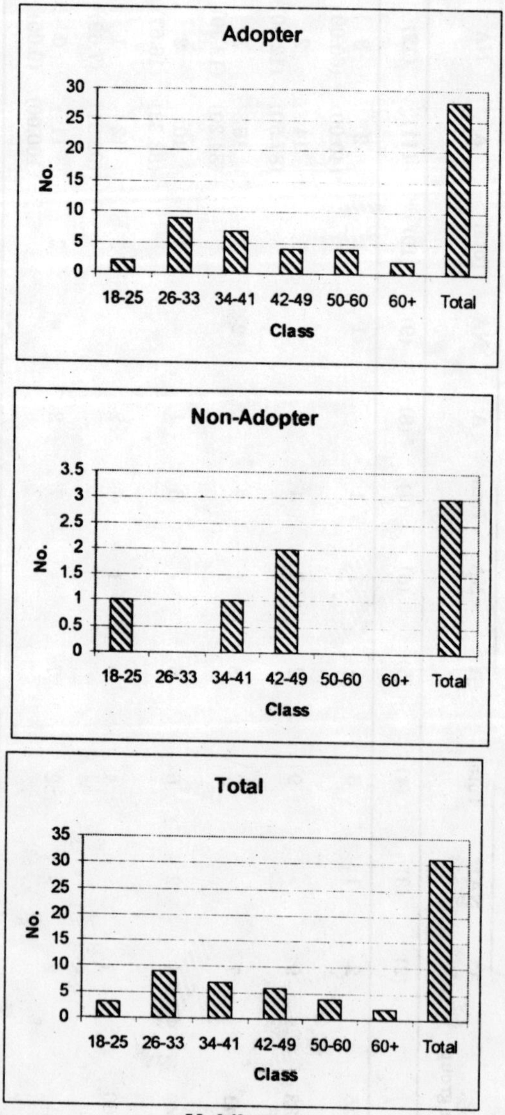

Kabilpur

Figure 4: Contd.

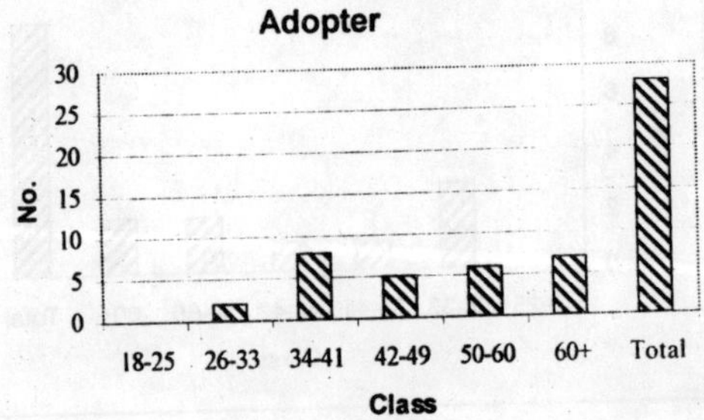

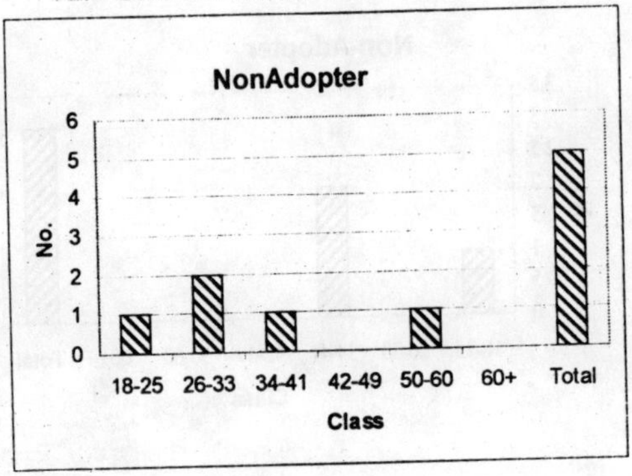

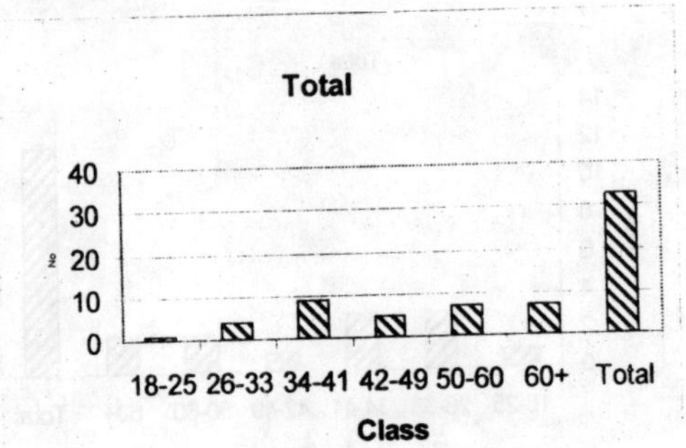

Latapakur

Figure 4: Contd.

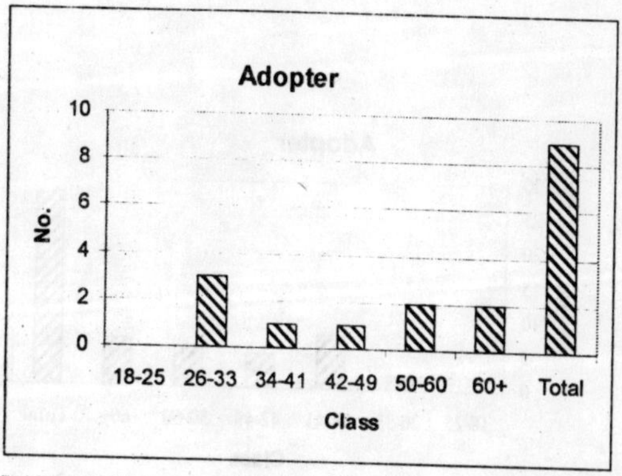

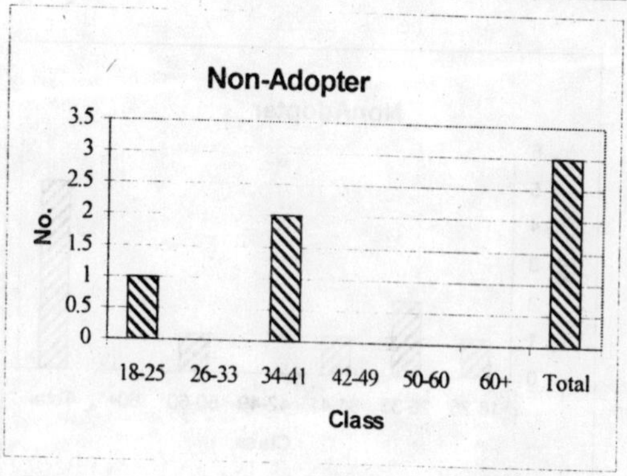

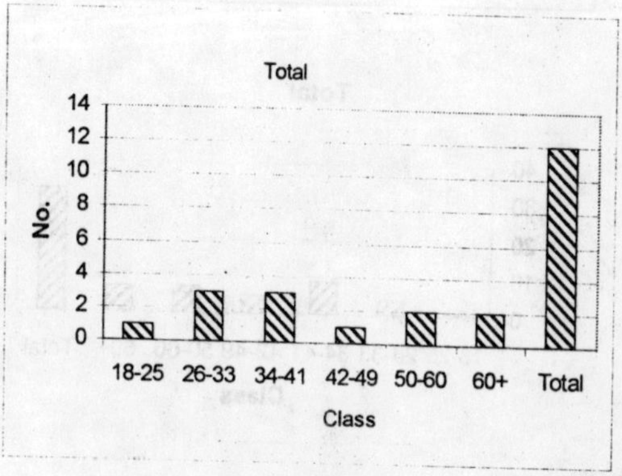

Bamundiha

Figure 4: Contd.

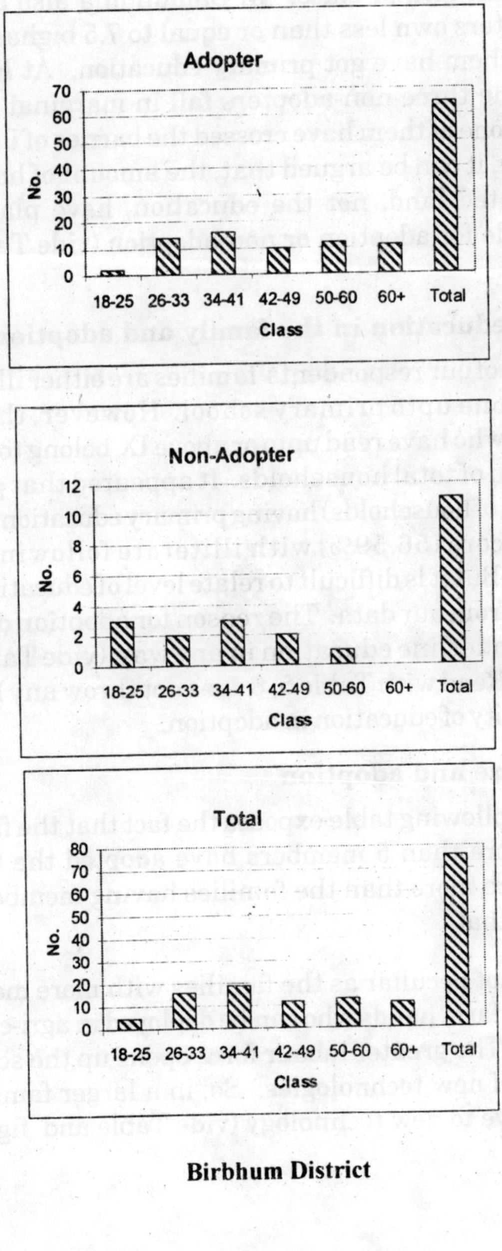

Birbhum District

At Latapakur all the 5 non-adopters have got their primary education, wholly or partially and 4 of them are in marginal farmer class. In Bamundiha also all the 3 non-adopters own less than or equal to 7.5 bighas of land and 2 of them have got primary education. At Kabilpur also all the three non-adopters fall in marginal farmers class and one of them have crossed the barrier of illiteracy. Therefore, it can be argued that, the amount of holding of the operated land, not the education, have played the crucial role for adoption or non-adoption (vide Table and figure 5).

Level of education in the family and adoption

Most of our respondents' families are either illite-rate or have gone upto primary school. However, the other members who have read upto or above IX belong to a small proportion of total households. It appeared that persons (not heads of households) having primary education had the highest score (56.59%) with illiterate following them (31.57%). But it is difficult to relate level of education with adoption from our data. The reason for adoption does not seem to underline education in any way (vide Table and figure 6). Read with Table 5, 6 does not throw any light on the causality of education in adoption.

Family size and adoption

The following table exposes the fact that the families having more than 5 members have adopted the technologies much more than the families having members 5 or less than that.

It is not peculiar as the families with more members have more farm hands who can be deployed in agri-cultural activities. The greater labour force opens up the scope for adoption of new technologies. So, in a larger family size is conducive to new technology (vide Table and figure 7).

Occupation and adoption

The nature and type of occupation is important factor of adoption of technology.

Among the respondent's main occupations, cultivation plays a vital role in adoption. These households may however, have secondary occupation or occupation allied to agriculture. That is how cultivator - sharecropper, cultivator - agricultural labourers as well as only cultivators are adopting new technology in agriculture (vide Table and figure 8).

Labour force and adoption

Let us now consider the number of persons engaged in agricultural activities, by households (Table 8). The majority of families (79.49%) having two persons engaged in agriculture adopted new technologies (79.49%), but they constitute 51.32% of the total households. Families having four and five persons engaged in agriculture are all adopters. Again it is also seen that household with a lone agricultural worker was also an adopter. But we cannot make any observation on the basis of this solitary case. It can therefore be safely said that more the number of persons engaged in agriculture, greater the possibility of adoption. This was also observed in previous discussion on family size (Table & figure 7).

Family type and adoption

Anthropologists often lay stress on the type of family in cases of their behaviour analysis. We also examined the family type vis-à-vis the adoption of technologies. Joint families as well as nuclear families are high adopters (according to Reddy and Murthy's terminology, Ibid).

With the number of respondents in our case we could not distinguish the influence of family type on adoption except taking note of the fact that joint families had higher score (vide Table & Figure 10).

Table 5: Distribution of respondents by education and different village

Village →	Kabilpur			Latapakur			Bamundiha			Grand Total		
Education	A*	NA**	Total	A	NA	Total	A	NA	Total	A	NA	Total
(1)	(2)	(3)	(4)	(5)	(6)	(7)	(6)	(9)	(10)	(11)	(12)	(13)
Illiterate	24	2	26	16	-	16	6	1	7	46 (93.88)	3 (6.12)	49(64.48) (100.00)
I - V	2	1	3	11	5	16	3	2	5	16 (66.67)	8 (33.33)	24(31.57) (100.00)
VI - VIII	2	-	2	1	-	1	-	-	-	3 (100.00)	0 (0.00)	3(3.95) (100.00)
Total	28	3	31	28	5	33	9	3	12	65 (85.55)	11 (15.45)	76(100.00) (100.00)

*A = Adopter
**NA = Non-adopter.
Source : Ibid

Figure 5: Distribution of Respondents by Education in Different Villages

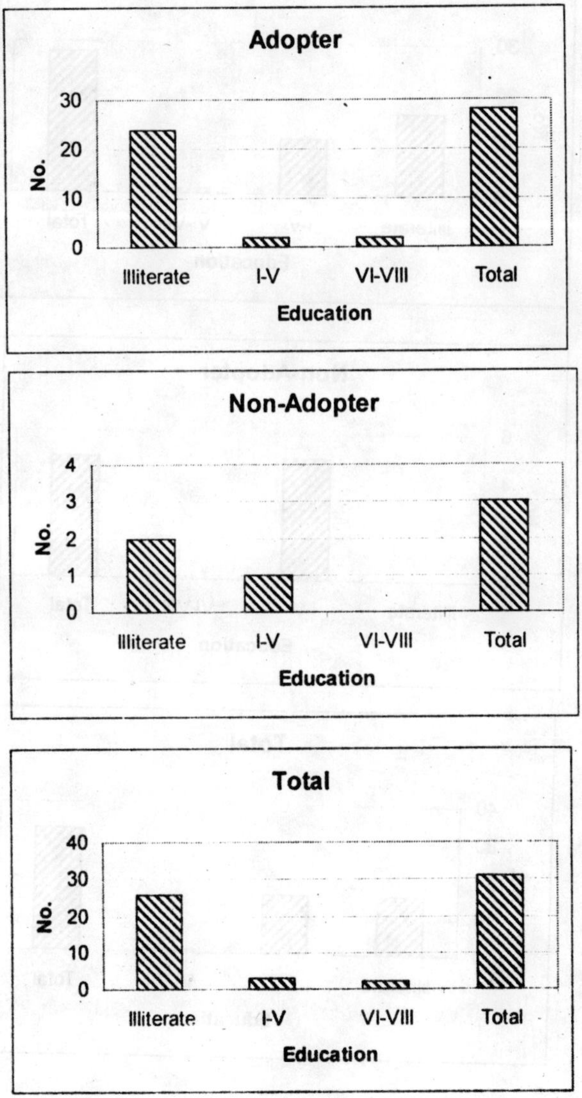

Kabilpur

Figure 5: Contd.

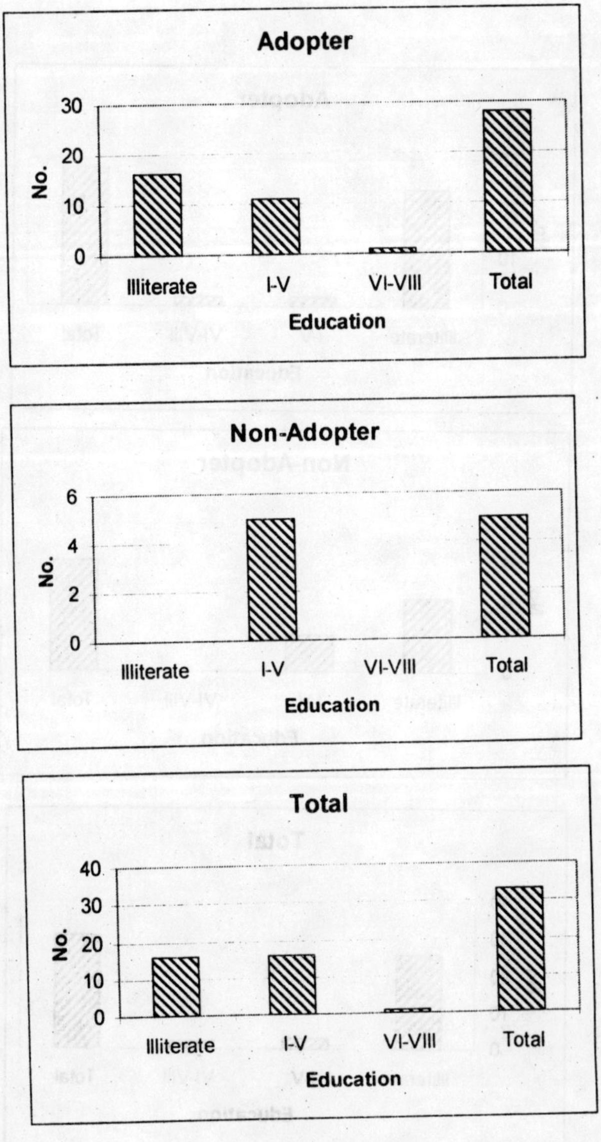

Latapakur

Figure 5: Contd.

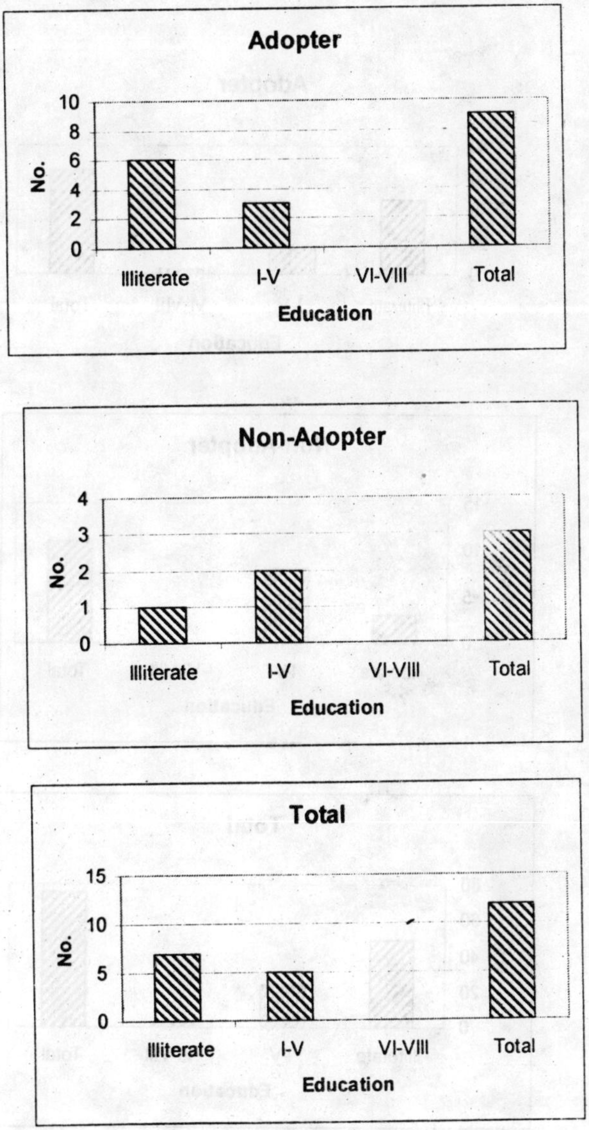

Bamundiha

Figure 5: Contd.

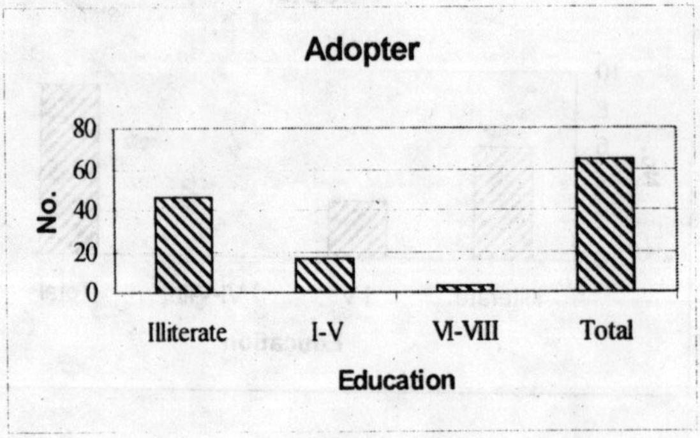

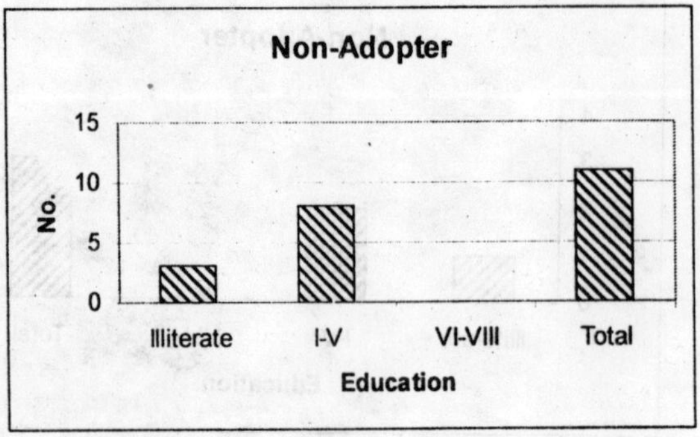

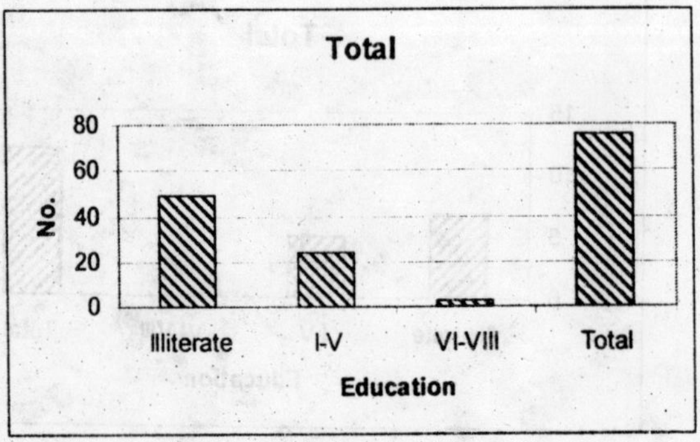

Birbhum District

Table 6 : Highest educated family members of the households and adoption.

Village →	Kabilpur			Latapakur			Bamundiha			Grand Total		
Highest Educated Family member	A*	NA**	Total	A	NA	Total	A	NA	Total	A	NA	Total
(1)	(2)	(3)	(4)	(5)	(6)	(7)	(8)	(9)	(10)	(11)	(12)	(13)
Illiterate	9	2	11	9	-	9	3	1	4	21 (87.50)	3 (12.50)	24(31.57) (100.00)
I - V	15	1	16	14	5	19	6	2	8	35 (81.40)	8 (18.60)	43(56.59) (100.00)
VI - VIII	3	-	3	3	-	3	-	-	-	6 (100.00)	0 (0.00)	6([illegible].89) (10[illegible].00)
IX - X	1	-	1	1	-	1	-	-	-	0 (0.00)	0 (0.00)	2(2.63) (100.00)
Above X	-	-	-	1	-	1	-	-	-	0 (0.00)	0 (0.00)	1(1.32) (100.00)
Total	28	3	31	28	5	33	9	3	12	65 (85.55)	11 (14.45)	76(100.00) (100.00)

*A = Adopter

**NA = Non-adopter.

Source : Ibid

Figure 6: Highest Educated Family Member of the Households and Adoption

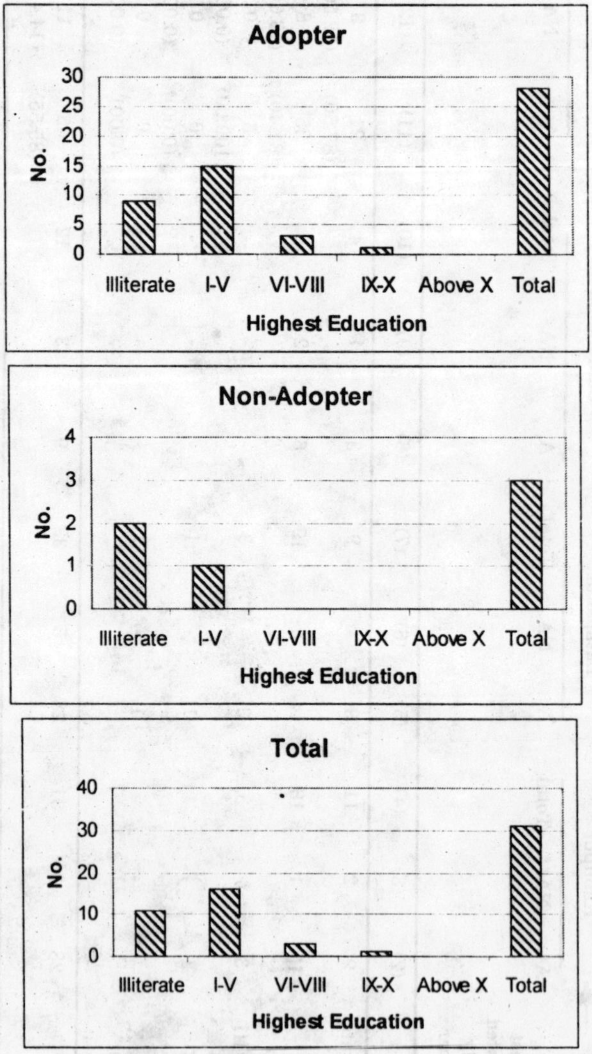

Kabilpur

Figure 6: Contd.

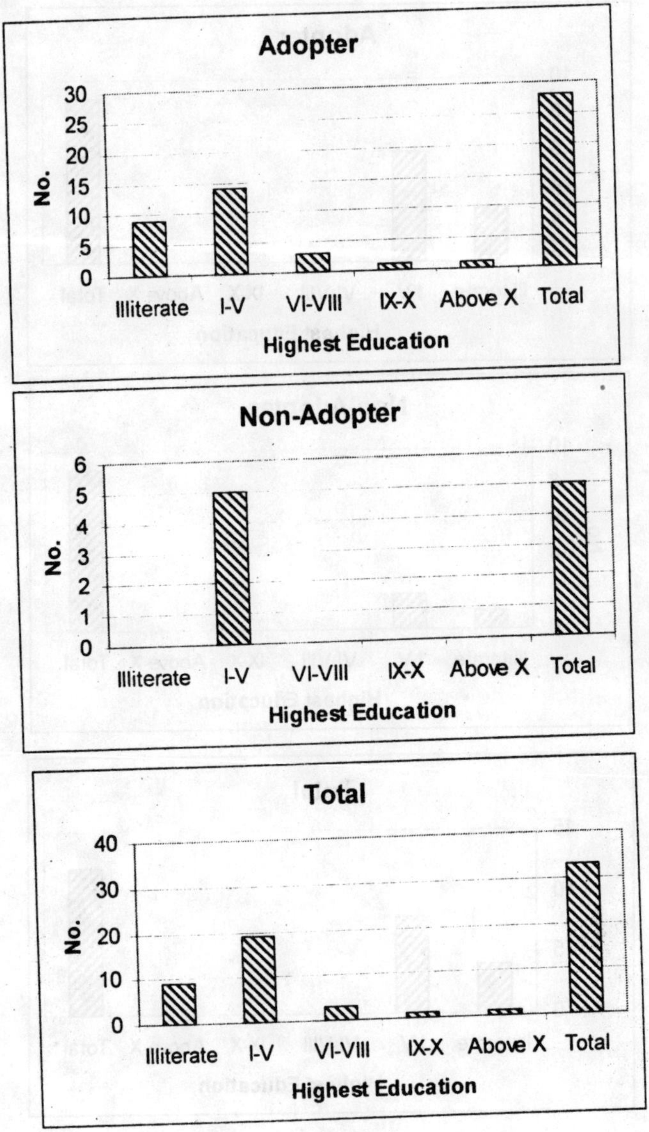

Latapakur

Figure 6: Contd.

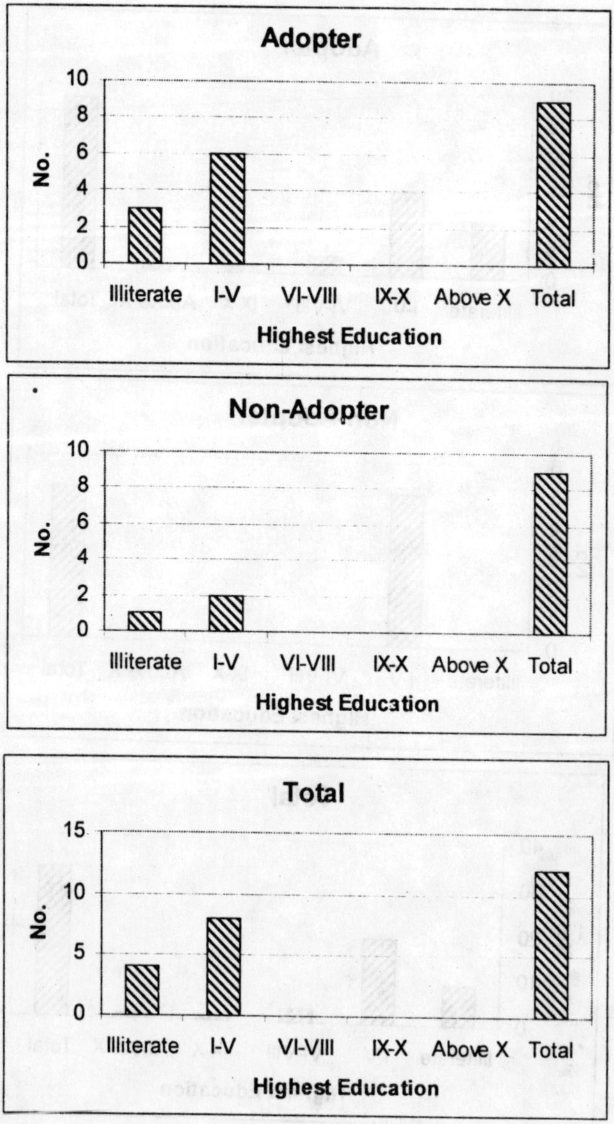

Bamundiha

Figure 6: Contd.

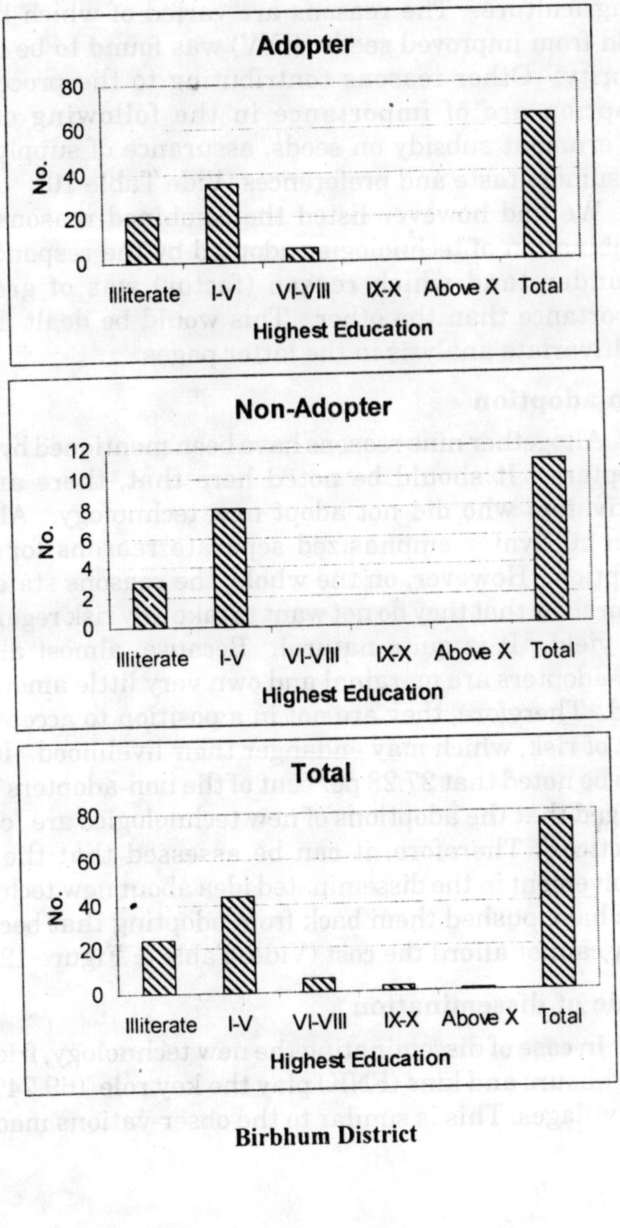

Birbhum District

Reasons for adoption

83.07% of respondents have exclusive reasons and 16.93% have combined reasons for adopting HYV seeds in agriculture. The reasons are varied of which better yield from improved seeds (HYV) was found to be of top priority. Other reasons contributing to the process of adoption are of importance in the following order; Government subsidy on seeds, assurance of supply and consumers taste and preferences (Vide Table 10).

We had however listed the combined reasons and combination of technologies adopted by the respondents to understand which reason (factor) was of greater importance than the other. This would be dealt in the multivariate analysis in the latter pages.

Non-adoption

Altogether nine reasons have been mentioned by non-adopters. It should be noted here that, there are 11 cultivators who did not adopt new technology. Almost each cultivator emphasized separate reasons for non-adoption. However, on the whole, the reasons stated by them show that they do not want to take any risk regarding the yield. It is quite natural. Because, almost all the non-adopters are marginal and own very little amount of land. Therefore, they are not in a position to accept any sort of risk, which may endanger their livelihood. It can also be noted that 27.28 per cent of the non-adopters have alleged that the adoptions of new technologies are 'costly practices'. Therefore, it can be assessed that the cost involvement in the disseminated idea about new technologies have pushed them back from adopting that because they cannot afford the cost (Vide, Table & Figure 12).

Mode of dissemination

In case of disseminating the new technology, friends, neighbours and kins (FNK) play the key role (69.74%) in our villages. This is similar to the obser-vations made by

Table 7 : Distribution of respondents by family size in different villages.

Village → Family Size	Kabilpur			Latapakur			Bamundiha			Grand Total		
	A*	NA**	Total	A	NA	Total	A	NA	Total	A	NA	Total
(1)	(2)	(3)	(4)	(5)	(6)	(7)	(8)	(9)	(10)	(11)	(12)	(13)
Up to 5	21	02	23	11	04	15	04	02	06	36 (81.82)	08 (18.18)	44(57.89) (100.00)
Above 5	07	01	08	17	01	18	05	01	06	29 (90.63)	03 (9.37)	32(42.11) (100.00)
Total	28	03	31	28	05	33	09	03	12	65 (85.55)	11 (14.45)	76(100.00) (100.00)

*A = Adopter
**NA = Non-adopter.
Source : Ibid

Figure 7: Distribution of Respondents by Family Size in Different Villages

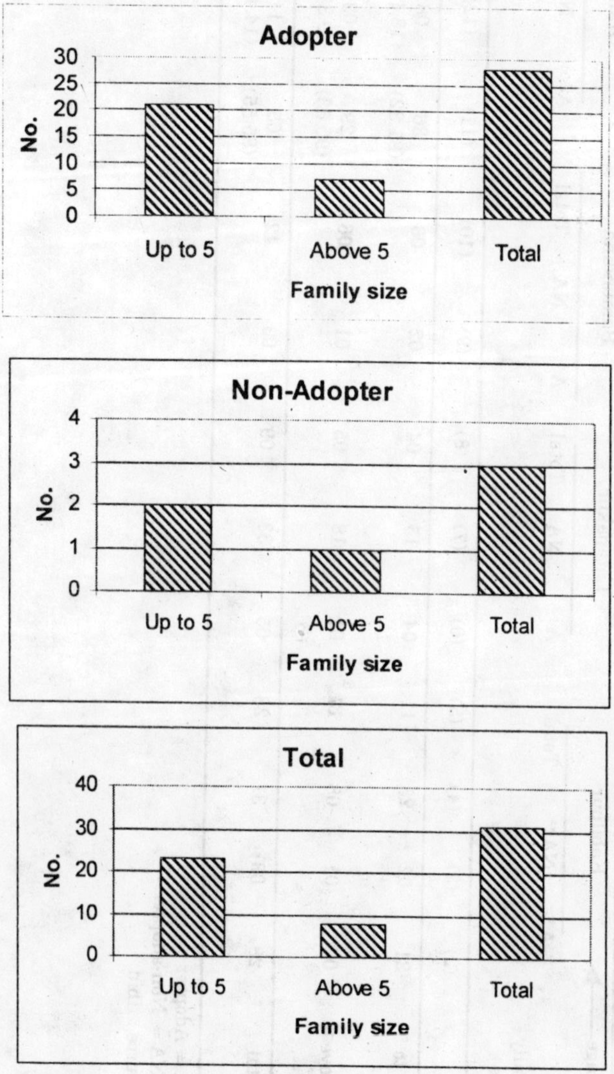

Kabilpur

Figure 7: Contd.

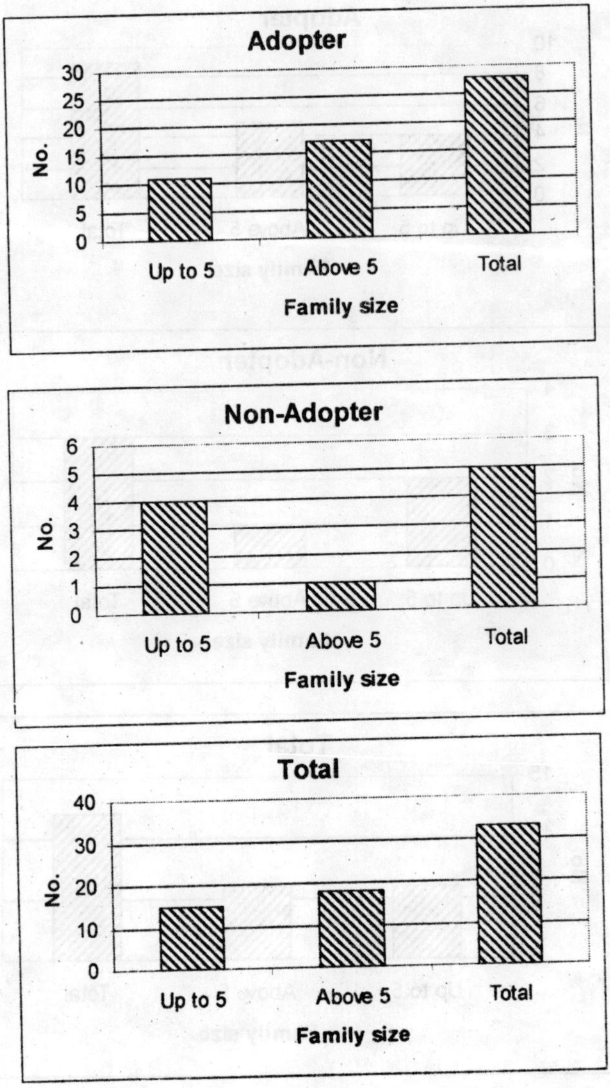

Latapakur

Figure 7: Contd.

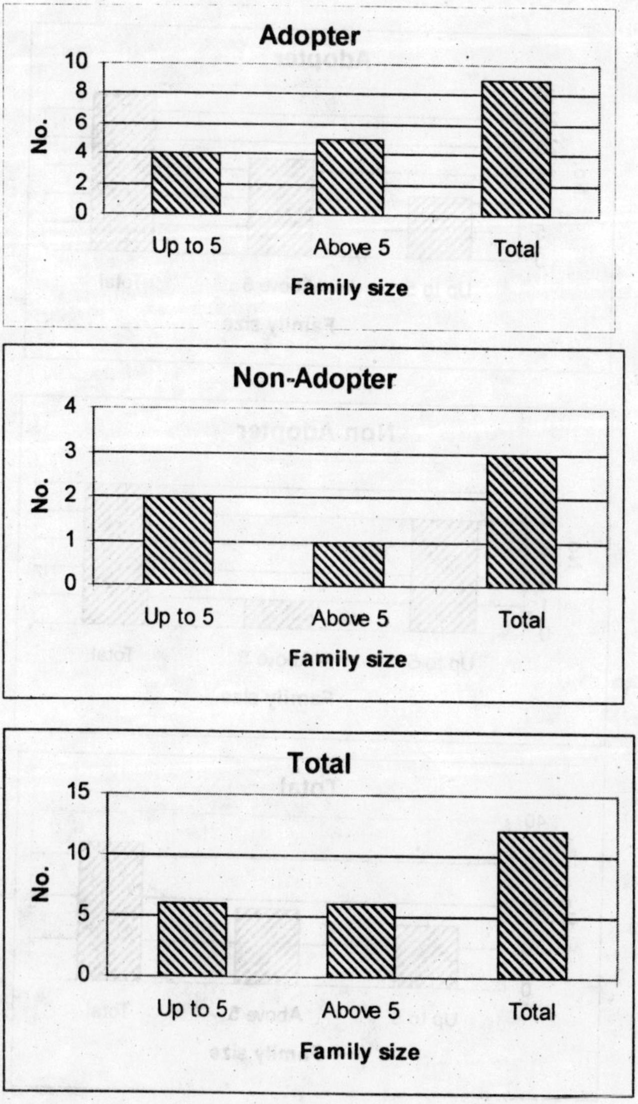

Bamundiha

Figure 7: Contd.

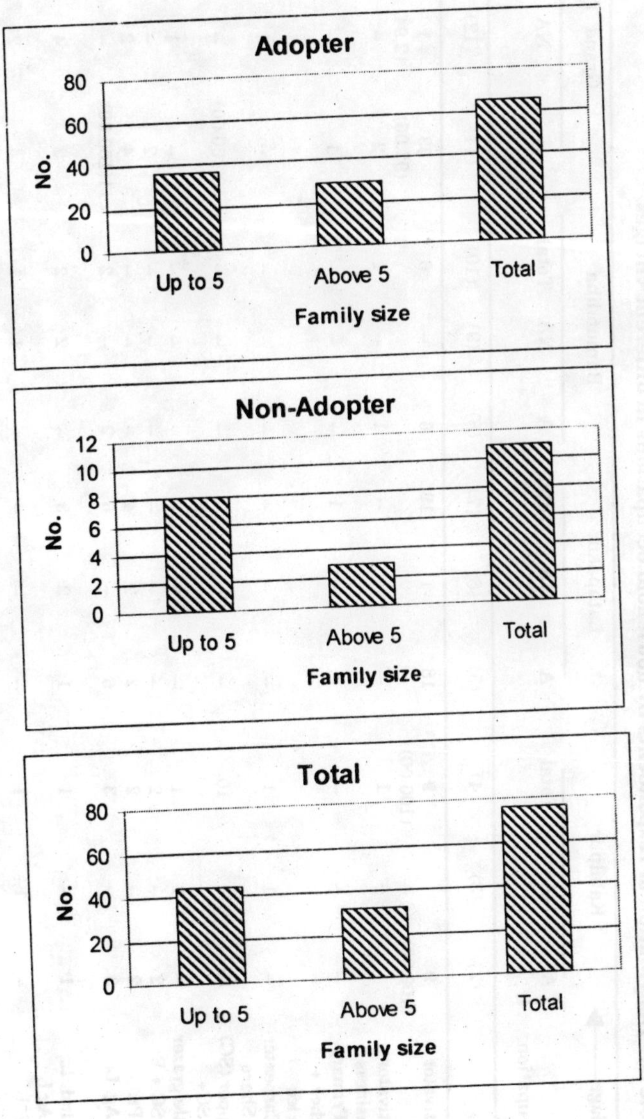

Birbhum District

Table 8 : Distribution of respondents by household occupations in different villages.

Village →	Kabilpur			Latapakur			Bamundiha			Grand Total		
Occupation	A*	NA**	Total	A	NA	Total	A	NA	Total	A	NA	Total
(1)	(2)	(3)	(4)	(5)	(6)	(7)	(8)	(9)	(10)	(11)	(12)	(13)
Cultivator (C)	9 (100.00)	--	9 (100.00)	18	1	19	6	--	6	33 (97.06)	1 (2.94)	34(44.74) (100.00)
Cultivator +Business	1	--	1	--	--	--	1	--	1	2	--	2 (2.63)
C +Primary teacher + Service	--	--	--	1	--	1	--	--	--	1	--	1 (1.32)
C+Carpenter	--	1	1	--	--	--	--	--	--	--	1	1 (1.32)
C + Share Cropper (SC)	10	--	10	--	--	--	--	--	--	10(100.00)	--	10(13.16)
C + SC+ Cattle grazer	--	1	1	--	--	--	--	--	--	--	1	1 (1.32)
C + SC + B	2	--	2	--	--	--	--	--	--	2	--	2 (2.63)
C + Pr.	2	--	2	2	2	4	--	--	--	4	2	6 (7.89)
C + Ag. L.	3	--	3	6	--	6	2	--	2	11(100.00)	--	11(14.47 (100.00)
C + Ind. L.	1	--	1	1	2	3	--	2	2	2	4	6 (7.89)
C + Ag.L. +Ind. L.	--	1	1	--	--	--	--	1	1	--	2	2 (2.63)
Total	28	3	31	28	5	33	9	3	12	65(85.55%)	11(14.45)	76(100.00)

*A = Adopter; **NA = Non-Adopter, Source: Ibid.

Figure 8: Distribution of Respondents by Household Occupations in Different Villages

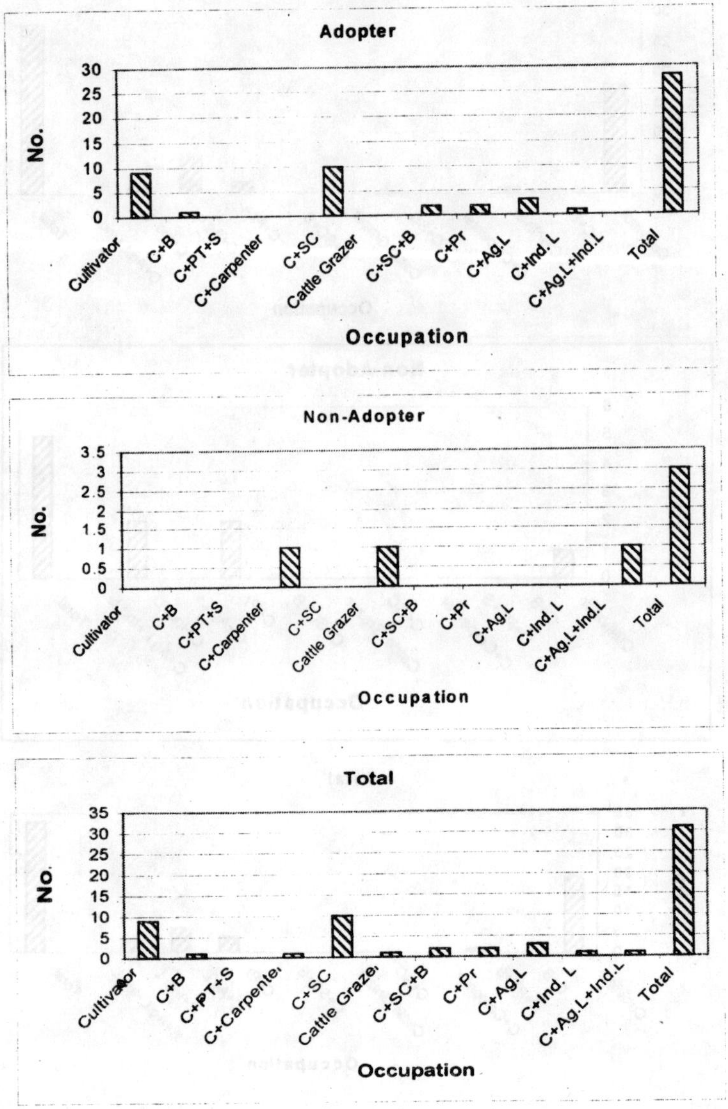

Kabilpur

Figure 8: Contd.

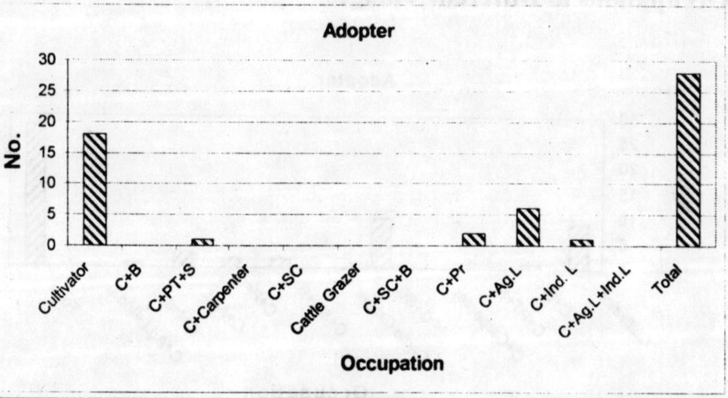

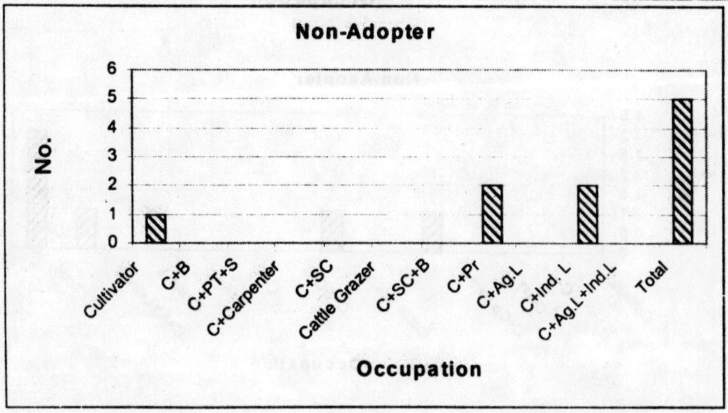

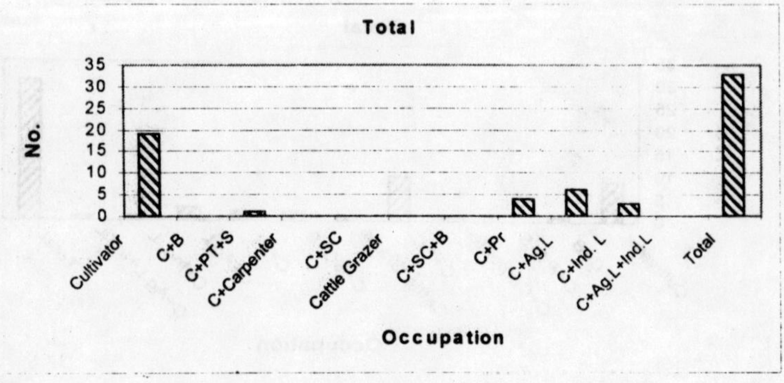

Latapakur

Figure 8: Contd.

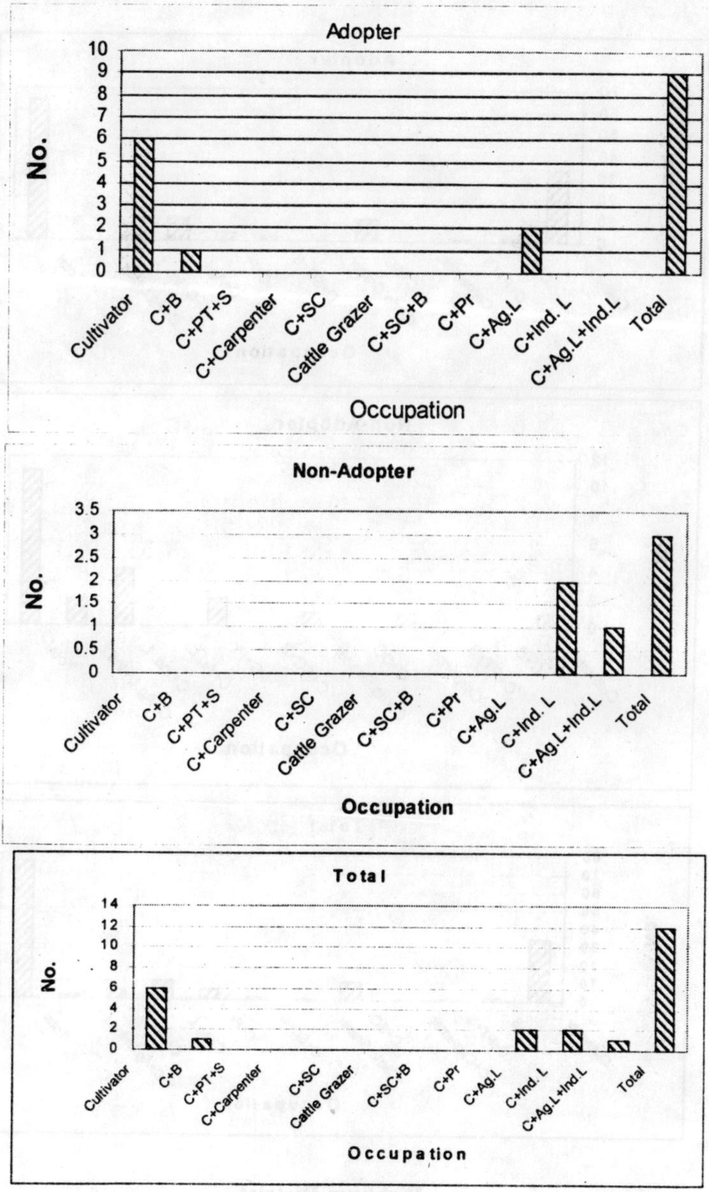

Bamundiha

Figure 8: Contd.

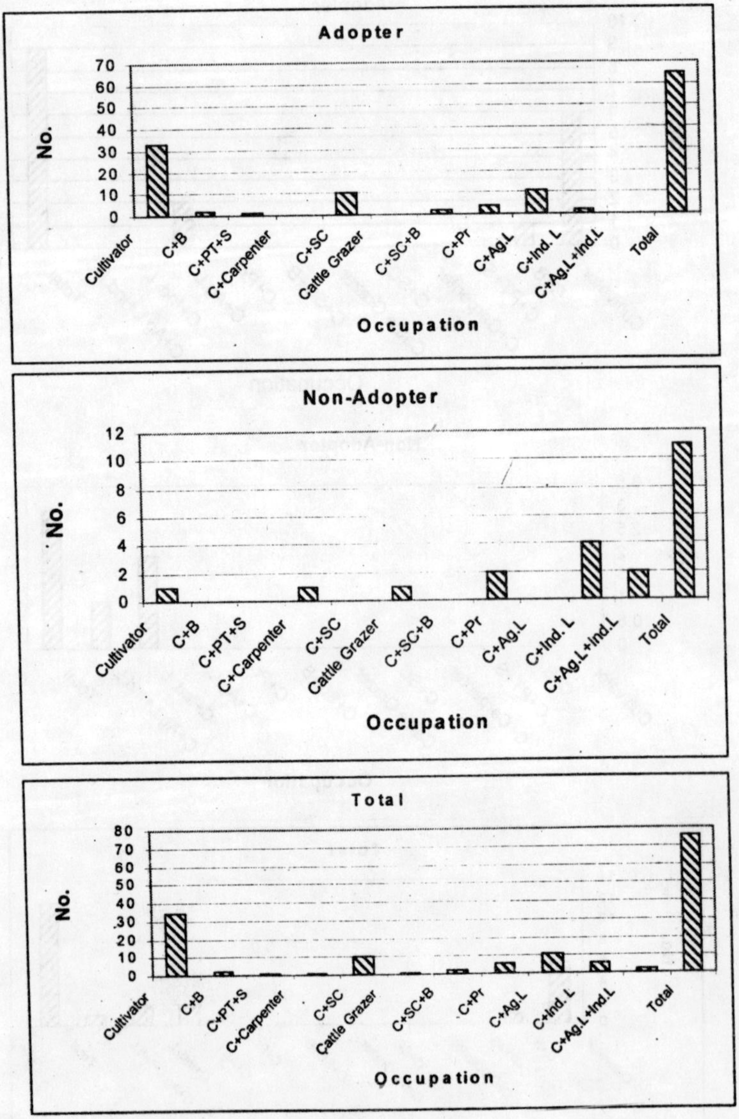

Birbhum District

Table 9 : Distribution of respondents by No. of persons engaged in agricultural activities.

Village →	Kabilpur			Latapakur			Bamundiha			Grand Total		
No. of Persons engaged	A*	NA**	Total	A	NA	Total	A	NA	Total	A	NA	Total
(1)	(2)	(3)	(4)	(5)	(6)	(7)	(8)	(9)	(10)	(11)	(12)	(13)
1	-	-	-	1	-	1	1	-	1	2 (100.00)	0 (0.00)	2(2.63) (100.00)
2	15	1	16	12	4	16	4	3	7	31 (79.49)	8 (20.51)	39 (51.32 (100.00)
3	8	2	10	7	1	8	4	-	4	19 (86.36)	3 (13.64)	22(28.95) (100.00)
4	5	-	5	6	-	6	-	-	-	11 (100.00)	0 (0.00)	11(14.47) (100.00)
5	-	-	-	2	-	2	-	-	-	2 (100.00)	0 (0.00)	2(2.63) (100.00)
Total	28	3	31	28	5	33	9	3	12	65 (85.55)	11 (14.45)	76(100.00) (100.00)

A = Adopter **NA = Non-adopter. Source: Ibid

Figure 9: Distribution of Respondents by the No. of Persons Engaged in Agricultural Activities

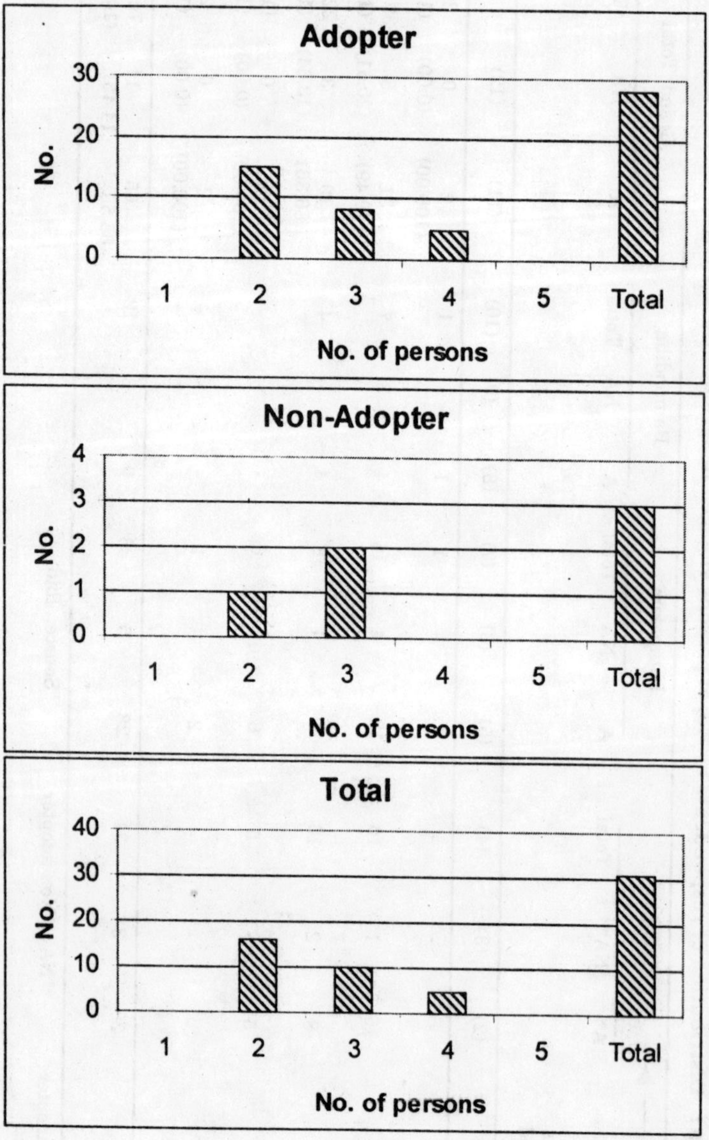

Kabilpur

Figure 9: Contd.

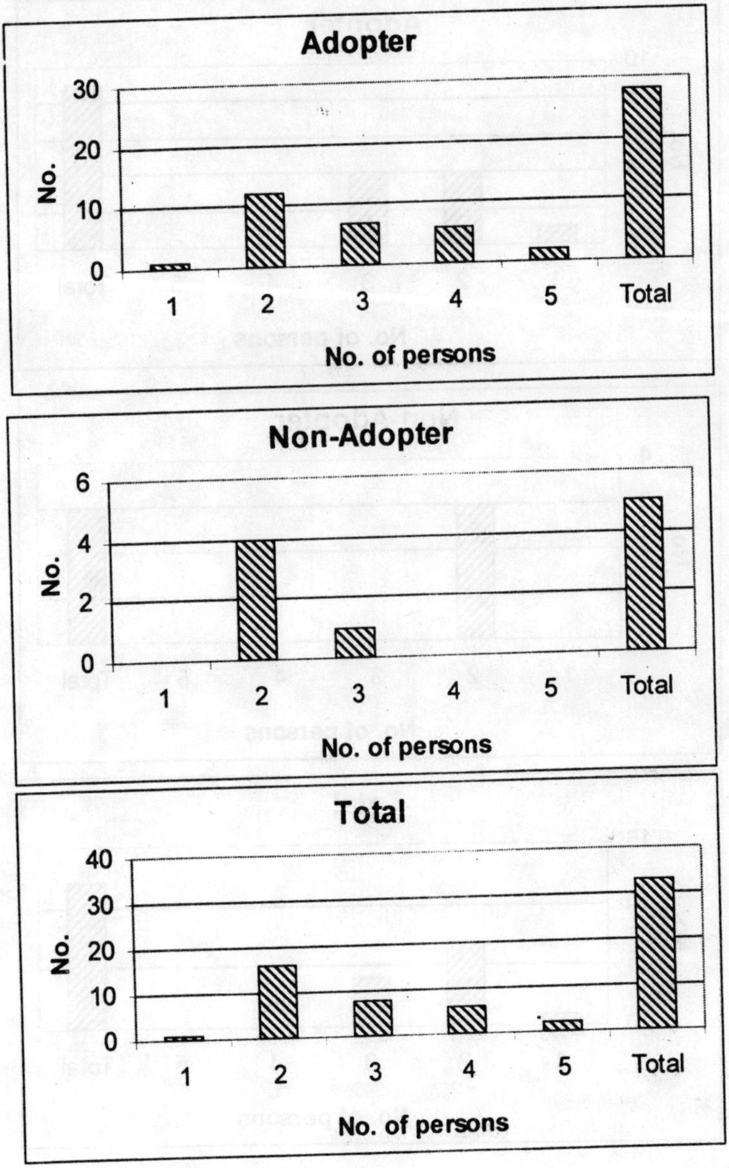

Latapakur

Figure 9: Contd.

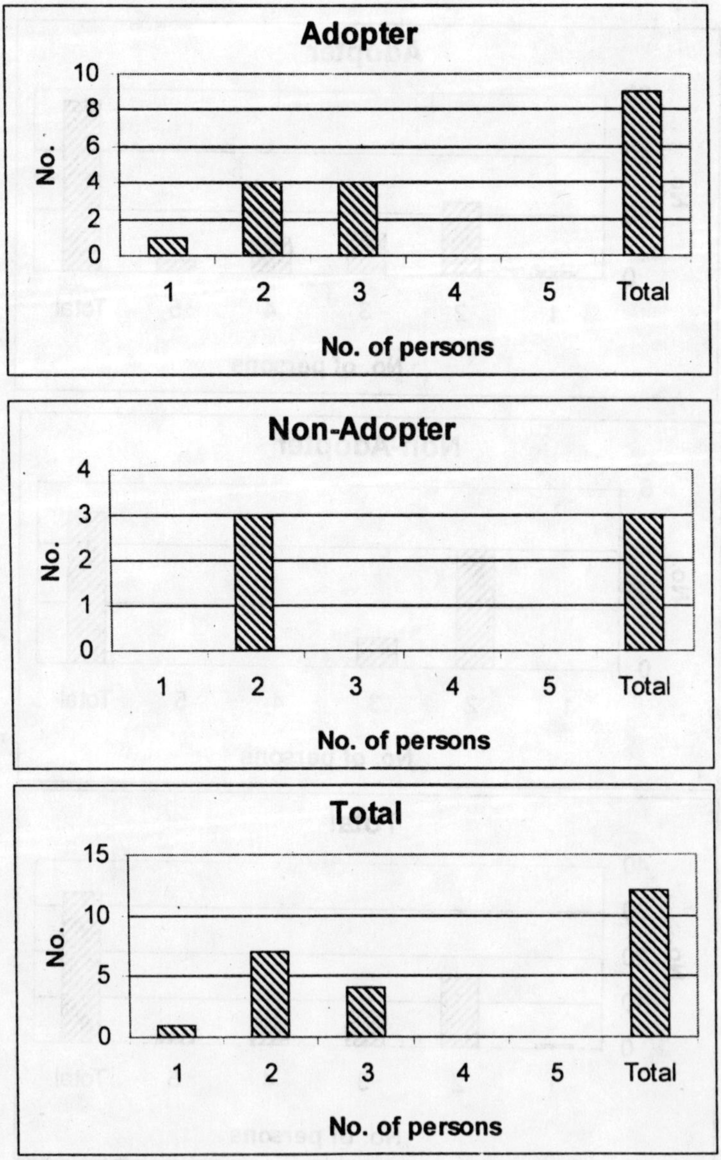

Bamandiha

Figure 9: Contd.

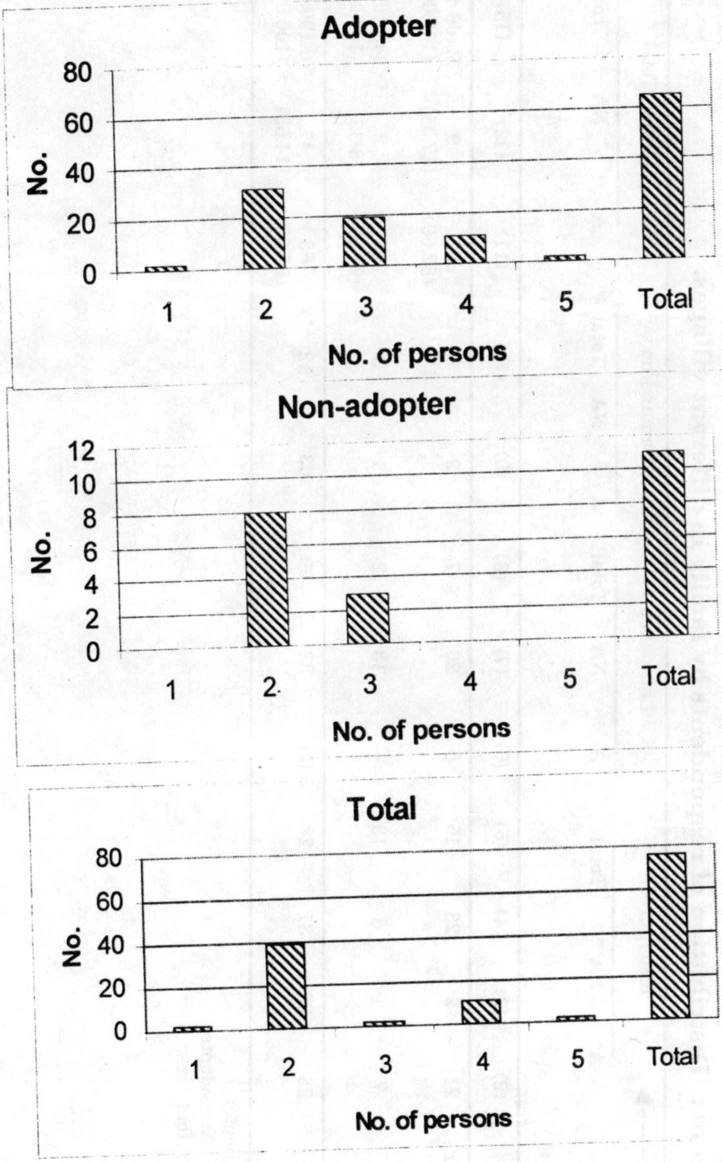

Birbhum District

Table 10 : Distribution of respondents by family in different villages.

Village ⟶	Kabilpur			Latapakur			Bamundiha			Grand Total		
Family Size	A*	NA**	Total	A	NA	Total	A	NA	Total	A	NA	Total
(1)	(2)	(3)	(4)	(5)	(6)	(7)	(8)	(9)	(10)	(11)	(12)	(13)
Nuclear	21	2	23	15	5	20	7	2	9	43 (82.69)	9 (17.31)	52(68.42) (100.00)
Joint	7	1	8	13	-	13	2	1	3	22 (91.67)	2 (8.33)	24(31.58) (100.00)
Total	28	03	31	28	05	33	09	03	12	65 (85.55)	11 (14.55)	76(100.00) (100.00)

*A = Adopter
**NA = Non-adopter.
Source : Ibid

Figure 10: Distribution of Respondents by Family in Different Villages

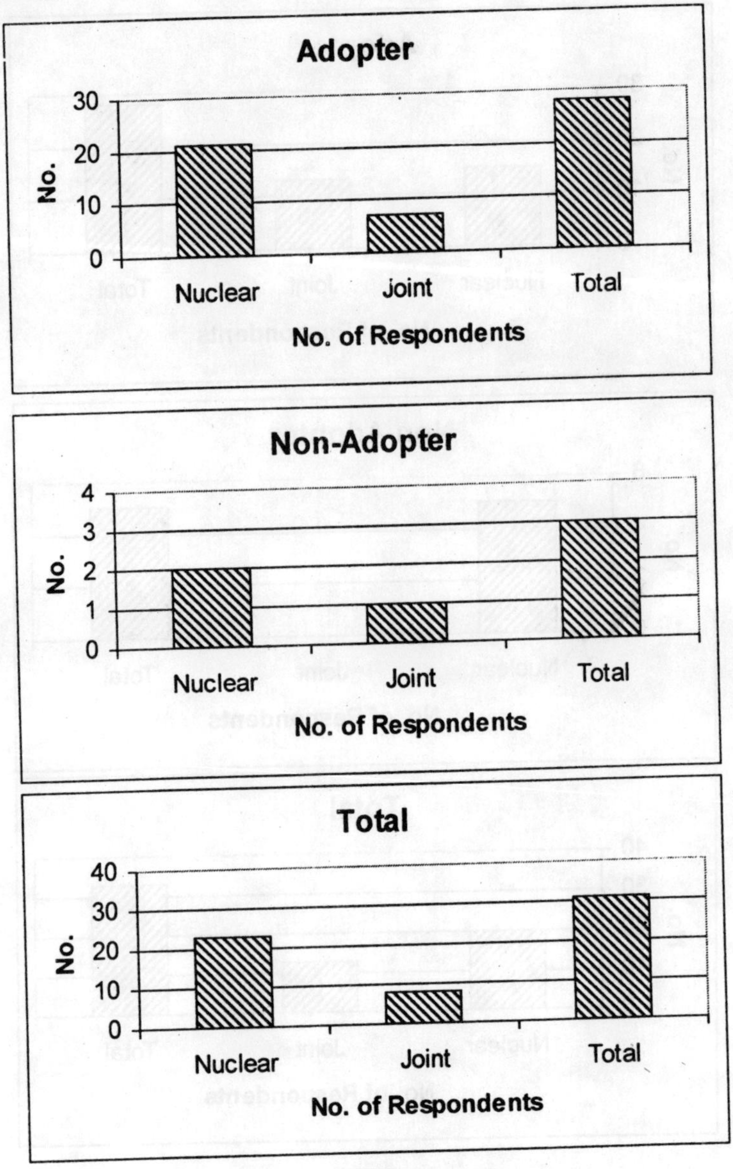

Kabilpur

Figure 10: Contd.

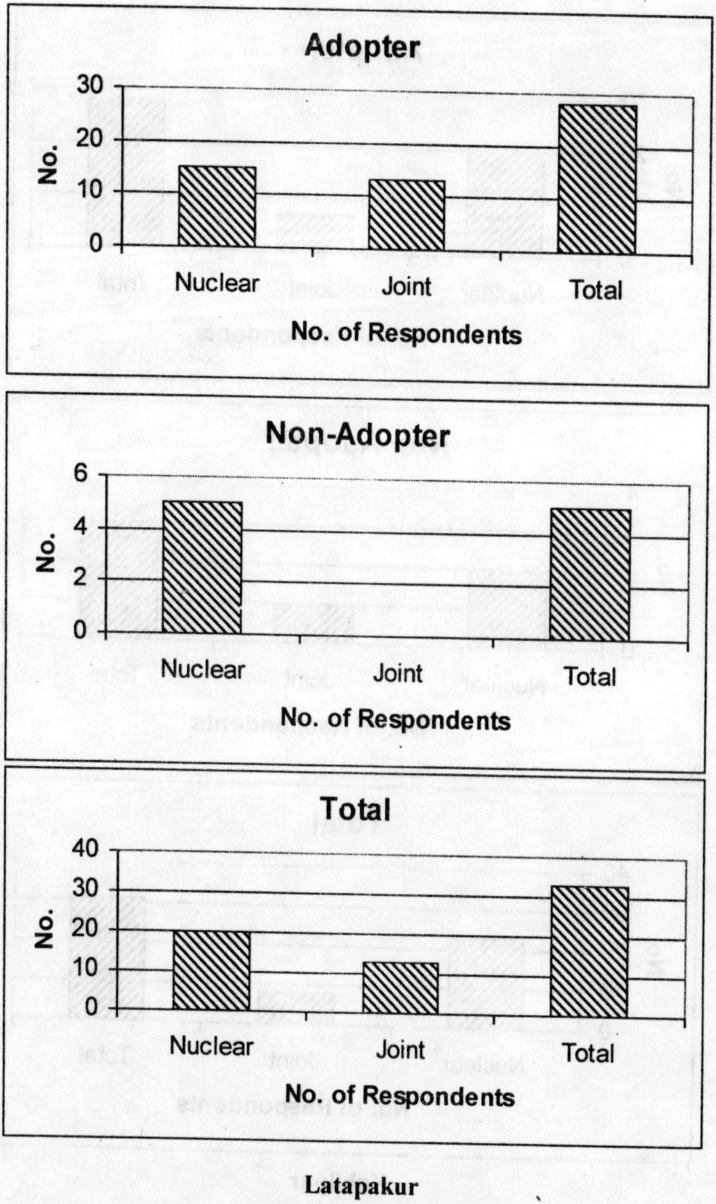

Latapakur

Figure 10: Contd.

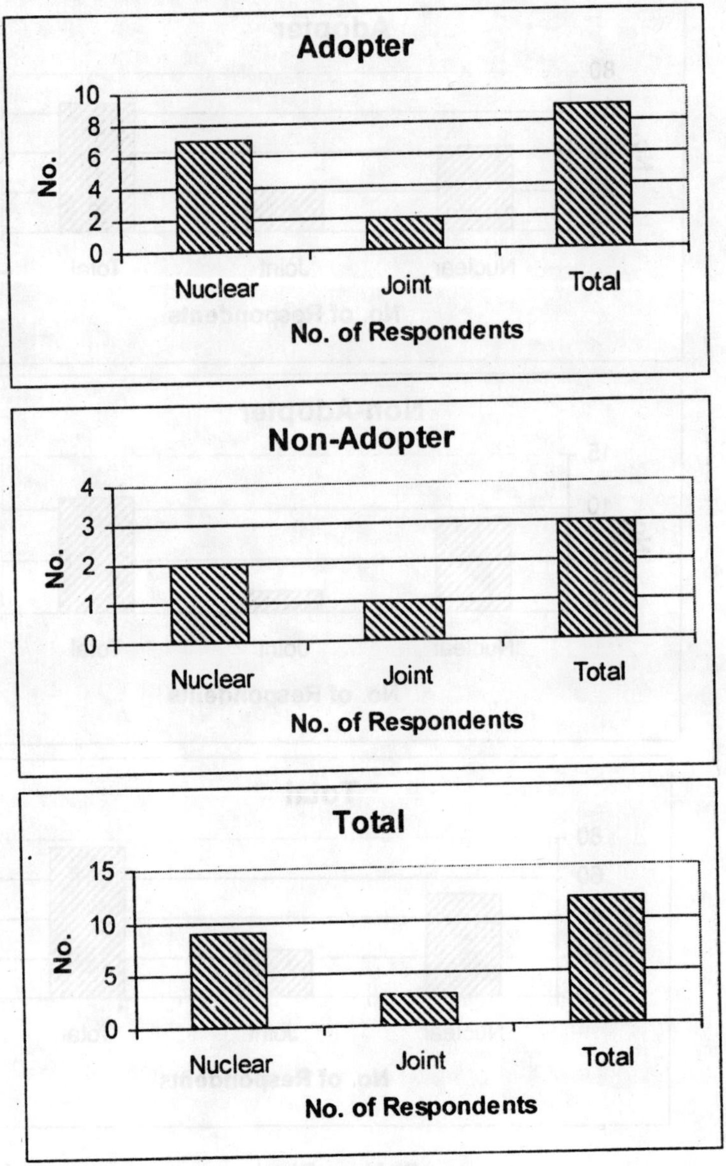

Bamandiha

Figure 10: Contd.

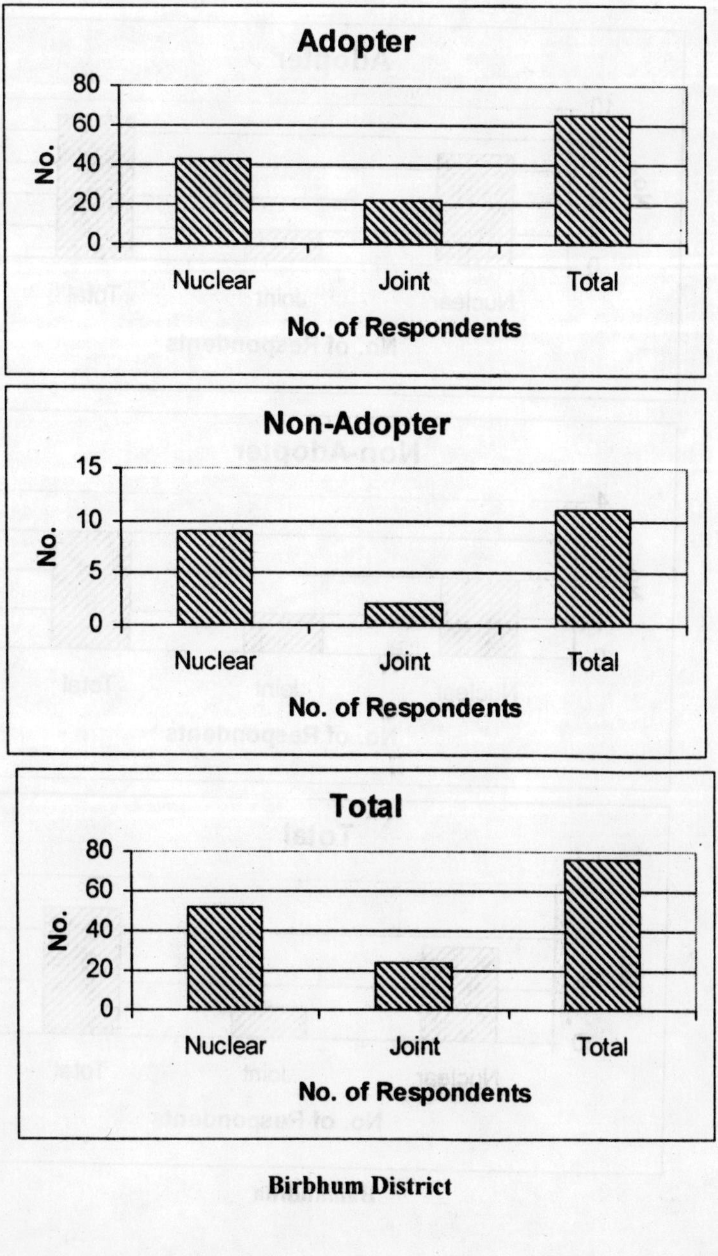

Birbhum District

the other researchers mentioned earlier. Government agencies (Statutory) played only marginal role (1.31%) and the voluntary agencies contri-buted a little (5.26%). None of the respondents was influenced exclusively by Statutory Agencies of Kabilpur and Bamundiha villages. In case of Bamundiha village, no voluntary agency operated (Vide, Table & figure 13).

Table 11: Reasons for adopting HYV Seeds by respondents in different villages

Reasons for adoption	Village			Total
	Kabilpur	Latapakur	Bamundiha	
(1)	(2)	(3)	(4)	(5)
Availability of seed	3 (60.00)	2 (40.00)	0 (0.00)	5 (7.69) (100.00)
Better yield	19 (51.35)	13 (35.14)	5 (13.51)	37 (56.92) (100.00)
Subsidised by the Govt.	1 (10.00)	8 (80.00)	1 (10.00)	10 (15.38) (100.00)
Sarnalagu is better to (Paddy) prepare the puffed rice	2 (100.00)	0 (0.00)	0 (0.00)	2 (3.08) (100.00)
Availability of seed and better yield	0 (0.00)	3 (100.00)	0 (0.00)	3 (4.62) (100.00)
Subsidised by the Govt. better yield	1 (16.67)	2 (33.33)	3 (50.00)	6 (9.23) (100.00)
Subsidised by the Govt. + Sarnalagu is better to prepare the puffed rice	2 (100.00)	0 (0.00)	0 (0.00)	2 (3.08) (100.00)
Total	28 (43.08)	28 (43.08)	9 (13.84)	65 (100.00) (100.00)

Source: Ibid.

Figure 11: Reasons for Adopting HYV Seeds by Respondents in Different Villages

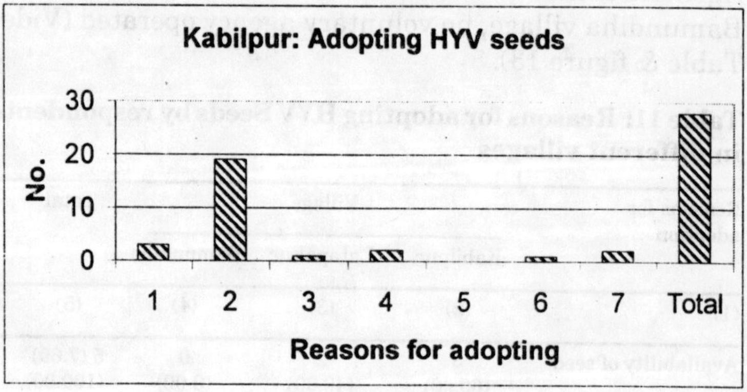

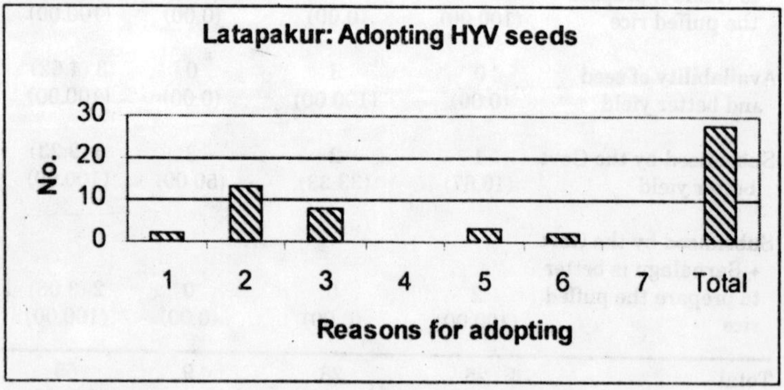

Figure 11: Contd.

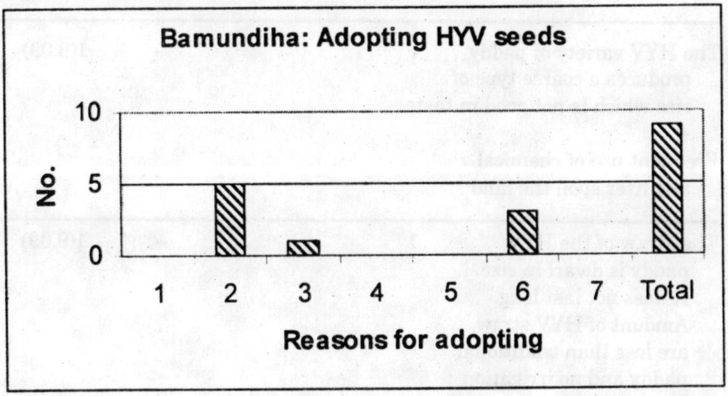

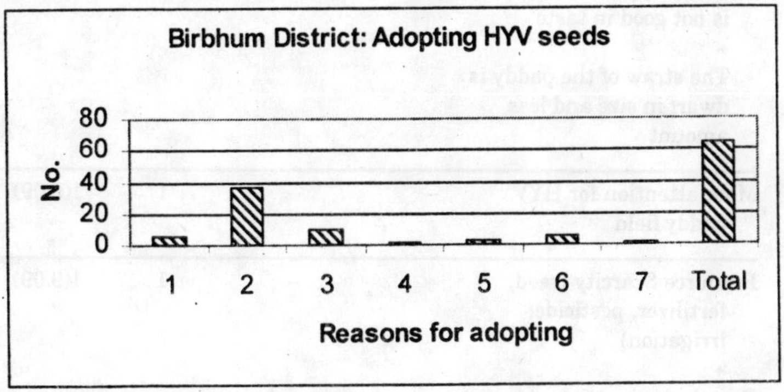

Table 12 : Reasons for non-adoption of new technology by respondents in different villages

Reasons for adoption	Village			Total
	Kabilpur	Latapakur	Bamundiha	
(1)	(2)	(3)	(4)	(5)
The HYV variety of paddy produces a coarse type of rice which is not good in taste + Frequent use of chemical fertilizer spoil the land	1	--	--	1(9.09)
The straw of the HYV paddy is dwarf in size. It does not last long. Amount of HYV straw are less than traditional paddy and no irrigation facility	1	--	--	1(9.09)
Frequent use of chemical fertilizer, spoil the land and no irrigation facility	--	1	--	1(9.09)
HYV paddy produces a coarse type of rice which is not good in taste + The straw of the paddy is dwarf in size and less amount	--	1	--	1(9.09)
More attention for HYV paddy field	--	--	1	1(9.09)
Resource Scarcity (seed, fertilizer, pesticide, irrigation) + Seasonal migration	--	--	1	1(9.09)
Resource scarcity (seed, fertilizer, irrigation)	--	1	--	1(9.09)

Table 12 : (contd.)

Reasons for adoption	Village			Total
	Kabilpur	Latapakur	Bamundiha	
(1)	(2)	(3)	(4)	(5)
Quality of available seed is not good (non-germinated seed) and no irrigation facility	1		--	1(9.09)
Need more attention +Costly practice	--	2	1	3(27.28)
TOTAL	3	5	3	11(100.00)

Figure 12: Reasons for Non-Adoption of New Technology by Respondents in Different Villages

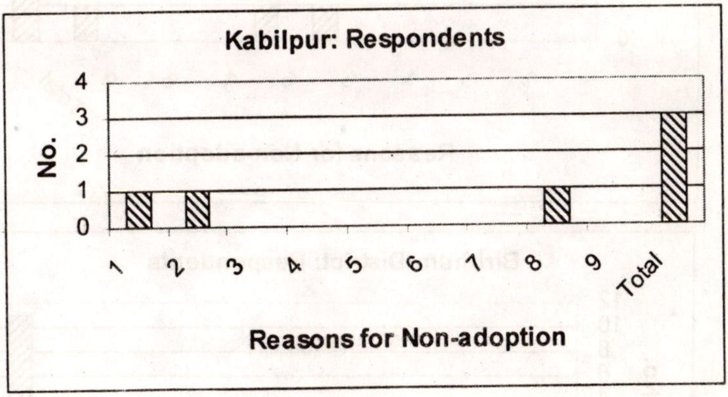

(contd.)

Figure 12: Contd.

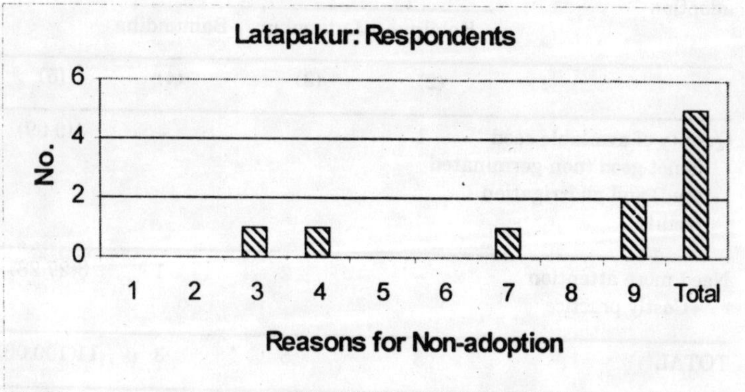

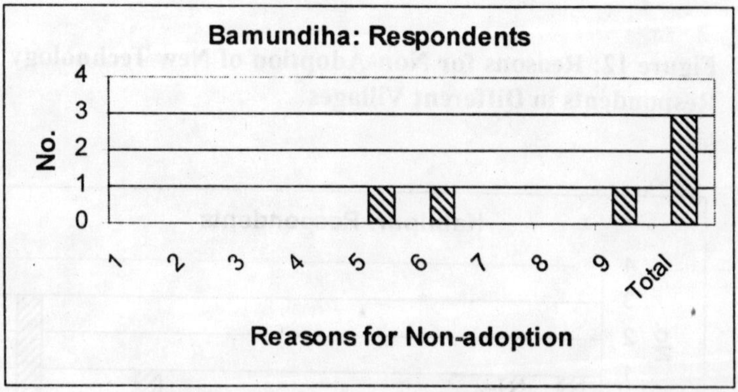

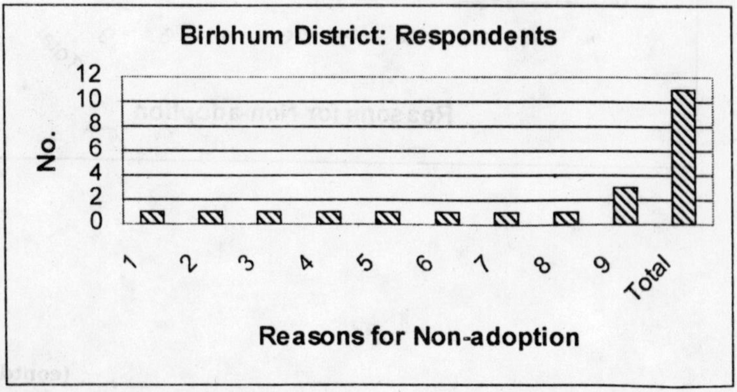

Table 13 : Dissemination of new technology by different Agents in different villages

Reasons for adoption	Village			Total
	Kabilpur	Latapakur	Bamundiha	
(1)	(2)	(3)	(4)	(5)
Statutory Agencies	0 (0.00)	1 (100.00)	0 (0.00)	1(1.31) (100.00)
Voluntary Agencies	2 (50.00)	2 (50.0C)	0 (0.00)	4 (5.26) (100.00)
FNK	18 (33.96)	24 (45.28)	11 (20.76)	53 (69.74) (100.00)
Statutory Agencies and FNK	5 (50.00)	4 (40.00)	1 (10.00)	10(13.16) (100.00)
Voluntary Agencies and FNK	6 (75.00)	2 (25.00)	0 (0.00)	8(10.53) (100.00)
Total	31 (40.79)	33 (43.92)	12 (15.79)	76(100.00) (100.00)

Source : Ibid

Figure 13: Dissemination of New Technology by Different Agents in Different Villages

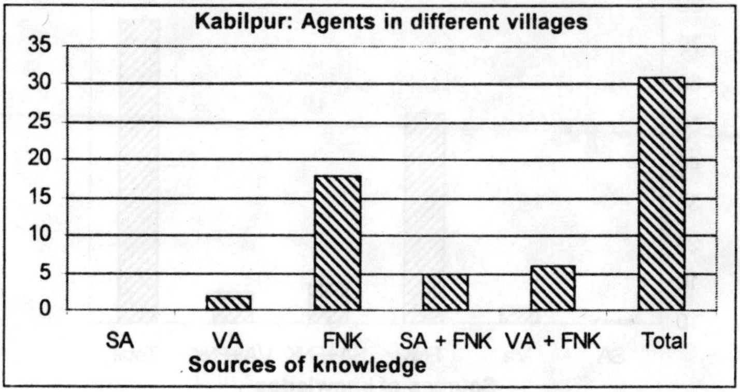

Figure 13: Contd.

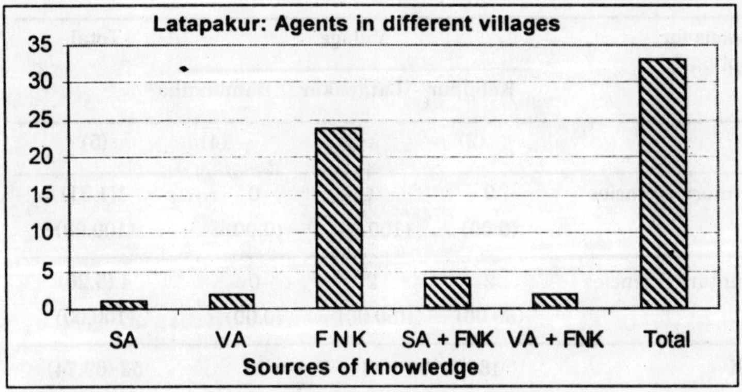

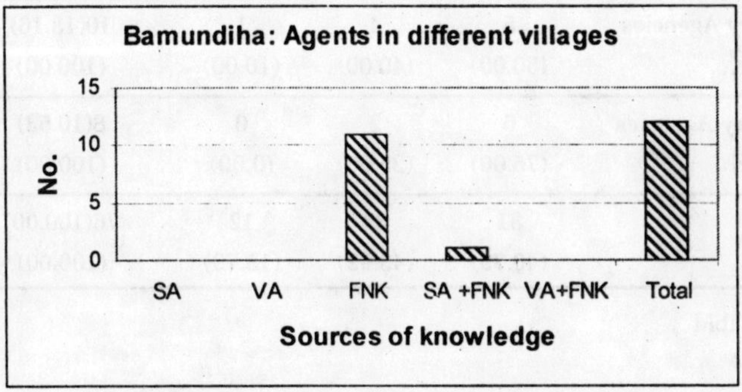

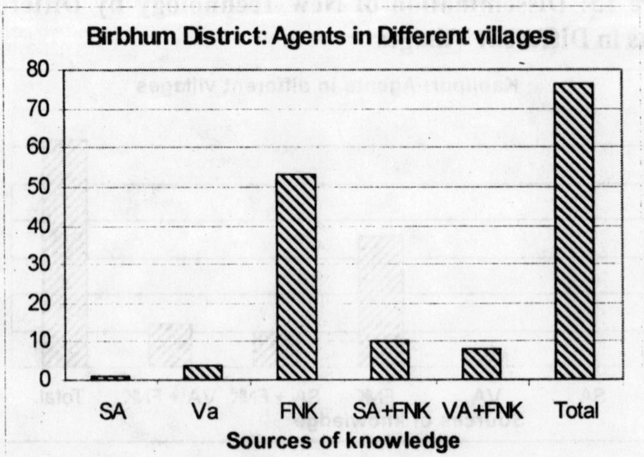

4

MULTIVARIATE ANALYSIS

In the aforesaid discussion, we tried to study the reasons and rate of adoption by categorizing the households. But these did not give us any unique pattern. The nature and characteristic peculiarities of the households' vis-a-vis the adoption therefore needed suitable statistical analysis.

We therefore listed all the technologies adopted for all households irrespective of their class, age, education, family size and village etc. 76 households and their adoption behaviour were therefore subjected to statistical analysis to understand the importance of specific reasons.

Hence, this multivariate analysis (Vide Tables 14 and 15).

For multivariate analysis here we have used Logistic Regression Model (1972) (Vide, BMDP Manual, 1990 version).

The model allows estimation of the effect of one group on the response variable in relation to the baseline group. The exponent of the regression coefficient shows the corresponding odds ratios. If the value of the odds ratio is greater than one then the effect on the response variable is more positive than that of baseline variable.

Six independent base variables are included in the analysis. Nuclear family for the type of family, minimum member's (i.e., up to 5) for family size, female for sex of head of household, the lowest educational group (i.e., illiterate) for educationof the respondent, the lowest educated members group in the family (i.e., illiterate) for highest education in the family, the lowest class (i.e., marginal) for farmers' class are taken as reference groups. All the variables are entered as categorical variables. The response is the following : "Adoption of new technology" values taken: Yes - 1 and No - 0.

Table 14 presents the estimated coefficients, and exp (coefficient) for various covariates under study. The result of stepwise logistic regression is shown in the subsequent table.

Joint family has no significant effect on adopting the new technology as compared to nuclear family. Family size has significant effect on adopting the new technology as compared to family size upto five. Sex has no significant effect on adopting the new technology as compared to female. Highest educated members in the family (i.e. I-X), has no significant effect as compared to illiterate.

It is interesting to note that among the educated respondents who are in the lower group have become more significant than those in higher groups. That is the respondents read upto class V have significant effect as compared to illiterates though respondents having read more than Class V - even having highest education - have no significance.

Table 15 reflects only the stepwise regression. It shows the kinds of technologies, which are most significant for the farmers so far, as the question of adoption is concerned. Among those who have adopted the technology, the risks of adopting ABCE, ABCG, ABCEG, ABCEFG, types of technologies were found to be most significant (Vide, Table 15).

It is seen that the exp (co-efficient) for a package ABCG is 0.1296. It is a package of four types of technologies i.e., use of improved seeds, fertilizers, pesticides and modern implements. Now if one type of technology is substituted by another keeping the number of types in one package unaltered, the exp (co-efficient) does not change. Even if there is any change, that can be regarded as minor one. Hence, for a package ABCE the exp (co-efficient) becomes 0.1296. It is same (upto four decimals) to the earlier package.

But as the number of types in a package is increased the exp (co-efficient) changes a lot. Thus for a package ABCEG the exp (co-efficient) is 0.1392 and for ABCEFG the exp (co-efficient) goes upto 0.1538. The change is quite distinctive.

The point worth noting here is that, with the increase in number in packages the relative risk of adopting the technologies increases. That is to say, if the cultivators are exposed to more packages, they are more prone to adopt those in their agricultural practices.

Table 14: Coefficients of Logistic regression of adoption of new technology on various socio-economic variables.

Variables →	All varieties		Stepwise	
Type of Family ↓	Coeff.	Exp. (Coeff.)	Coeff.	Exp. (coeff.)
(1)	(2)	(3)	(4)	(5)
Nuclear[R*]	---	---	---	---
Joint	-0.4039	0.6677	---	---
Up to 5[R]	---	---	---	---
Above 5	0.1662	1.1808	---	---

(contd.)

Variables → Type of Family ↓	All varieties Coeff.	Exp. (Coeff.)	Stepwise Coeff.	Exp. (coeff.)
(1)	(2)	(3)	(4)	(5)
Sex				
Female[R]	---	---	---	---
Male	0.2971	.7430	---	---
Education	---	---	---	---
Illiteratre[R]				
I-V	0.0883	1.0924	---	---
VI-VIII	-0.6310	0.5320	---	---
Highest education in the family	---	---	---	---
Illiterate[R]				
I-V	-0.0562	0.9454	---	---
VI-VIII	-0.0121	0.9880	---	---
Above VIII	-0.3316	0.7178	---	---
Economic Class (Land size)				
Marginal[R] ($\leq$ 7.5 Bigha)	---	---	---	---
Small (7.6 to 15.0 Bigha)	-0.6228	0.5364	-0.5762	.5620
Large (15.1 and above)	-0.4417	0.6430	---	---
X^2	8.83		5.02	
d.f.	10		1	

*R = Reference group. Source : Survey data (1992-93).

Table 15 : Importance of packages of new technology by the adopters.

Variables	Stepwise	
	Coefficient	exp coefficient
(1)	(2)	(4)
New Technologies : Use of improved seeds, fertilizer, pesticides and modern implements (ABCG)	-2.0431	0.1296
Use of improved seeds, fertilizer, pesticides, irrigation (ABCE)	-2.0431	0.1296
Use of improved seeds, fertilizer, pesticides, irrigation and modern implements (ABCEG)	-1.9719	0.1392
Use of improved seeds, fertilizer, pesticides, irrigation, modern practice and modern implements (ABCEFG)	–1.8723	0.1538
X^2		
d.f.		

*Vide note A & B.
Source : Ibid

NOTE A
Name of technology

A = use of improved seed

A_1 = cereals (paddy, wheat)

A_2 = pulses

A_3 = vegetables

A_4 = oil seeds (Mustard)

B = use of fertilizer

C = use of pesticide

D = use of herbicide

E = irrigation

F = modern practice

F_1 = line sowing

F_2 = line of top dressing

F_3 = weeding (mechanical)

F_4 = three ploughing

F_5 = transplantation

F_6 = distance of heel

F_7 = No. of seedlings per heel

F_8 = wet seed bed

G = modern implements

G_1 = plough (Mould board plough)

G_2 = hoe- weeding

G_3 = tractor (Disc plough, time plough)

G_4 = diesel pump (portable)

G_5 = paddy thresher

G_6 = liquid spray machine

G_7 = duster spray machine

NOTE B

For the analysis of Cox regression model, we have grouped the types of technology in the following way.

A = Use of improved seed (HYV)

AB = Use of improved seed (HYV) and Chemical fertilizer.

AE = Use of improved seed (HYV) and irrigation.

ABC	=	Use of HYV seed, Chemical fertilizer and Pesticide.
ABE	=	Use of HYV, Chemical fertilizer and irrigation.
ABF	=	Use of HYV seed, Chemical fertilizer and modern practice.
ABG	=	Use of HYV seed, Chemical fertilizer and modern implements.
ABCG	=	Use of HYV seed, Chemical fertilizer, Pesticide and modern Implementations.
ABCE	=	Use of HYV seed, Chemical fertilizer, Pesticide and irrigation.
ABCFG	=	Use of HYV seed, Chemical fertilizer, Pesticide, Modern practice and Modern implements.
ABCEG	=	Use of HYV seed, Chemical fertilizer, Pesticide, Irrigation and Modern implements.
ABCEFG	=	Use of HYV seed, Chemical fertilizer, Pesticide, Irrigation, Modern practice, Modern implements.
B	=	Use of Chemical fertilizer.
BC	=	Use of Chemical fertilizer and Pesticide.
BG	=	Use of Chemical fertilizer and Modern implements.
BCG	=	Use of Chemical fertilizer, pesticide and modern implements.

5

SUMMARY, FINDINGS AND SUGGESTIONS

From the analysis of the tables, we could identify the influence of certain factors contributing to the process of adoption in all the three villages. The amount of land holding is of prime importance for adopting the new technologies. The education level, sex, family size or the types of the families have certainly their effects when they are considered in case of particular respondent. But for the households as a whole of whom majority is small and marginal farmers, the effects of sex, age, education, and family size are marginal and only the control on land holding becomes the major factor. Beca-use we found almost all the non-adopters belonged to marginal farmers group, which has very little land.

It is evident from the multivariate analysis that when the partial effects of all the variates come to play simultaneously, they produce certain combined effect. It is observed that with respect to nuclear family joint families have no significant effect or education has no significance as compared to illiteracy. This finding also corroborates the analysis and assessment that were made in the text.

The marginal farmers generally do not want to take any risk involved in adopting any new technology. It is observed that most of the farmers become aware of the new idea through FNK. But that information does not assure them of success in their new venture.

Most of the non-adopters have argued 'more attention' was needed for new technology which they could not provide. At the same time they have alleged that the practice is costly and beyond their means. Therefore whatever is their social-status, the marginal farmers simply shrink back from adopting new techno-logies only due to their vulnerable economic-status.

The farmers in 'small' category have responded well like the 'large' ones. Because their economic-status have allowed them to test the new technologies.

Another interesting thing is the number of technologies adopted by them. It is seen that higher the number in packages higher is the rate of adoption. Again, it can be argued that as the number in the packages increases the cost of the packages escalates. That again goes beyond the reach of the farmers who are already in poor state. That's why the marginal farmers allege against the 'costly practice'. It may also be assumed that closer the source of propagators of modern technologies greater will be the rate of adoption. We gained this insight from the discussion with the villagers.

Personal sources of information of both institutional and non-institutional types have greater credibility with farmers than impersonal sources. However, it is seen that the rate of adoption of new technologies is quite high. Because out of 76 respondents altogether 65 respondents have adopted new technologies. Again, bulks of marginal farmers (34 out of 44) have also adopted the same. Some marginal farmers are dropped out, because if the land holding is the only constraint, then all the marginal farmers should have responded in same way - i.e., negatively. But that has not occurred. So there might be other factors combined effect of which may be responsible for non-adoption by particular households.

In almost all the cases it is observed that 2 to 3 members of each family are engaged in agriculture. At Bamundihə village, all the marginal farmer households engage 2-3 members of their families in land. For the non-adopters the holding is only 2-4 bighas whereas for the adopters it was between 5-7 bighas. At Latapakur village, the non-adopters own land amounting 0.5 to 2 bighas, but they also engage at least 2 members of their families. This is an indicator of 'disguised unemploy-ment' or 'under employment' in the villages under study.

To sum up, it can be said that, for disseminating the new technologies the amount of land holding should be given prime stress. At the same time it should also be noted that under-employment is also an inhibitive factor towards adoption of technology.

The behaviour of tribal farmers in adoption of technology was not different from that of the non-tribal farmers studied elsewhere by erstwhile scholars as well as by the present researcher. It was rather the class difference among the tribals that influenced the ability to adopt new technology. So, in order to get the technology adopted by the farmer, it is imperative that the technology should be of very low cost and suitable to the taste and preference of the farmers, be they tribal or non-tribal.

The above discussions naturally lead to the following suggestions:

1. The dissemination process is much more important to make the tribals exposed to new scientific agricultural practices. It should be of regular and organised nature so that, the hitherto unfocussed and yet most potential segment of agrarian population could get an easy access to knowledge and practices. Hence, an institution like Krishi Vigyan Kendra for training of practicing farmers and their children should have been established in Birbhum district long ago. The farming skill of the tribals have to be improved and presence of such an institution is extremely useful for formu-lation of suitable agronomic as well as practices allied to agriculture. It is satisfying to note that such an institution Rathindra Kristhi Vigyan Kendra has been Pallicharcha Kendra (Viswa Bharati), Bolpur Santiniketan.
2. Research work of the Agricultural University at Srinikitan, Birbhum should include technologies appropriate to the socio-economic situation of the tribals in the area. Labour intensive technologies should be preferred in contrast to the capital-intensive techno-logies in order to tackle the problem of unemployment.

   The fruits of reforming and mechanizing agriculture should percolate to this downtrodden section at faster rate so that they are boosted up in psyche and attitude.

Therefore, we would like to draw attention of the social and agricultural scientists as well as the agencies both governmental and non-governmental levels to the present need of the tribal societies. We did not find tribals as 'Laggards' contrary to the common belief that they preferred to remain in a closed society. We found that with the change in the circumstances, they are also keen on coming out of stagnation and are seeking more production for their own benefits. They are equally interested in adopting new ideas as the non-tribals are. If the policy formulations do not keep these under consideration and the tribals are blamed for no fault on their own by the dispensing authorities there would be gross miscarriage of natural justice.

BIBLIOGRAPHY

1. Acharya, Hemlata. (1956). Urbanization role of a one-lakh city. Sociological Bulletin, 5(2).

2. Adler, Davi. (1955). An Analysis of Quality in the Associated Public School Systems Through a Study of the Patterns of Diffusion of Selected Educational Practices, Ph.D Thesis, N. Y., Teachers College, Columbia University.

3. Allen, Harley Earl. (1956). The Diffusion of Educational Practices in the School Systems of the Metropolitan School Study Council, Ph.D. Thesis, N. Y. Teachers College, Columbia University.

4. Anderson and Marvin A and others. (1965). An Appraisal of Factors Affecting the Acceptance and Use of Fertilizer in Iowa 1953, Ames, Iowa Agriculture Experiment Station, Special Report 16.

5. Armstrong, Joseph B. (1959). Country Agent Activities and the Adoption of Soil Building Practices, Ph.D. Thesis, Lexington, University of Kentucky.

6. Bardhan, Pranab (ed.). (1989). The Economic Theory of Agrarian Institutions. Oxford: Clarendon Press.

7. Barrington Thomas M. (1953). The Introduction of Selected Educational Practices into Teachers Colleges and Their Laboratory Schools, N. Y., Columbia University Teachers College, Bureau of Publications.

8. Barton, Allan. (1961). Unpublished Data N.Y., Columbia University, Bureau of Applied Social Research.

9. Biggs, S. D. (1990). A multiple source of innovation model of agricultural research and technology promotion: World Development 18, PP. 1481-1499.

10. Biggs, S. D. Farrington, J. (1991). Agricultural Research and the Rural Poor: A review of Social Science Analysis. Ottawa: International Development Research Centre.

11. Bose, Santipriya. (1961). Characteristic of Farmers Who Adopt Agriculture Practices in Indian Villages in Rural Sociology, 26:138-45

12. Bose, Santi Priya and Satadal Dasgupta (1962). The Adoption process. Calcutta : Department of Agriculture, Government of West Bengal.

13. Bose, S. P., S. Dasgupta and S. P. Das. (1962). A study into the uses of Deep tubewell water in the Barasat Region of West Bengal, Calcutta : Socio-Agro-Economic Research Organization. Department of Agriculture, Government of West Bengal.

14. Bowmers, Raymord V. (1938). Differential Intensity of Intra-Societal Diffusion. American Sociological Review, 3:21-31.

15. Caplow, Theodore. (1952). Market Attitudes: A Research Report from the Medical Field, Harvard Business Review, 3, 21-31.

16. Chapin, F. Stuart. (1928). N.Y. Century. The original statement of the S-shaped adopter distribution, in Cultural Change.

17. Clark, N. and Clay. E. (1968). The drylad research project at Indore, 1974-80 an institutional innovation in rural technology transfer; Journal of Rural Studies, 3, PP. 157-173.

18. Coeking, Walter. (1951). The Regional Introduction of Educational Practice in Urban School Systems in the United States, N. Y. Teachers College, Columbia University, Institute of Administrative Research Study.

19. Dasgupta, Satadal. (1989). Diffusion of Agricultural Innovations in village India, Willey Eastern Limited.

20. Davis, Alice. (1966). Technicways in American Civilization. Social forces, 18: 317-330.

21. Dexter, Lewis Anthony and White, David, M. (1964). People, Society and Mass Communication (edited). New York; The Free Press.

22. Donaldson. G. F. and Melnerney, J. P. (1973). Changing machinery, technology and agricultural adjustment, American Journal of Agricultural Economics 55, PP. 829-839.

23. Dube, S. C. (1958). India's Changing Villages: Human Factors in Community Development. London: Routledge and Kegan Paul.

24. Fligel, Frederick, C. (1967). Literacy and Exposure to Agricultural Information: A Comparison of Some Indian and Brazilian Data. Behavioural Sciences and Community Development, 1 : 89-99.

25. Gallup, George. (1955). The absorption Rate of Ideas. Public Opinion Quarterly, 19: 234-242.

26. Ghosh, Bhola Nath. (1992). Field Level Research: Some of our experience, in Folklore, PP. 162-167, Sept-Oct., Calcutta.

27. Ghosh, Bhola Nath. (1992). Diffusion of Technology in Agriculture, in Journal of the Indian Anthropological Society, no. 27, PP. 123-130, Calcutta.

28. Ghosh, Bhola Nath. (1994). Social network of decision making in farming systems: An exploratory study in Rural Areas, in Connection, Development of Sociology, University of South Carolina, vol. 17, Issue 2, PP. 61-74, Oct. Columbia. U.S.A.

29. Ghosh, Bhola Nath. (1995). Pleasure of Field work: Some of our experiences, in Socialist Perspective, Vol. 22, no. 3-4, PP 176-184, December 1994- March 1995, Calcutta.

30. Ghosh, Bhola Nath. (1996). Rural leadership and Development, Mohit Publications, 3305, Delhi Gate, New Delhi.

31. Ghosh, Bhola Nath. (1997). Relevance of Adages in Agricultural Practices: A Sociological Approach, in Social Science perspectives in Agriculture edited by D. Das gupta & Siddhartha D. Mukhopadhyay, PP. 42-46, published by Institute of Agricultural, (Palli Sikha Bharana), Visva-Bharati, Sriniketan.

32. Ghosh, Bhola Nath. (1997). The Theories of diffusion: Some empirical observations on Agricultural Activities in Rural Areas, in Indian Journal of Regional Science, Vol. xxix, number 2, PP. 1-17, 1997, Calcutta

33. Ghosh, Bhola Nath. (1998). Some experience of diffusion adoption in rural societies, in South Asian Anthropologist, Vol. 19 (1), PP 31-36, March, Ranchi, Bihar.

34. Ghosh, B.N. & K. Bandhyopadhya. (2000). "Need for Transfer of Technology Through Panchayati Raj System: An Observation' in Welfare, Choice and Development (Essays in Honour of Professor Amartya Sen), PP 129-139, Kanishya Publishers, Distributors, New Delhi.

35. Ghosh, B.N. & T.S.Vasulu. (2001). "Indicators of Socio-economic Status of Tribal Populations in India" in Socio-economic Development in India (ed), Vol.II, PP 420-484, Mohit Publications, New Delhi.

36. Gist, N. P. and Fayj, S. F. (1965). Urban Society, New York: Jhamas Y. Crownell.

37. Gostch, C. H. and McEachron, M. B. (1983). Technology Choice and Technological change in Third World Agriculture: concepts, empirial observations and research issues, In Lucas, B. A. and and Freedman, S. (eds.) Technology Choice And Change In Developing Countries, Dublin: Tycooly, PP. 29-62.

38. Hoffer, Charles R. (1942). Acceptance of Approved Farming Practices among Farmers of Dutch Descent, East Lawsing. Michigan Experiment Station Special Bulletin, 316

39. Janardhan Rao, R. (1987). Land alienation in tribal areas: Kakatiya University, Warangal.

40. Jones. (1967). The adoption and diffusion of agricultural practices, World Agricultural Economics and Rural Sociology Abstract, 9.

41. Katz, Elihu. (1961). The Social Itinerary of Technical Change: Two Studies on the Diffusion of Innovation, Human Organization, 20, 70-82.

42. Katz (1961), Elihu and Martin L Levin. (1959). Traditions of Research on the Diffusion of Innovation, paper presented at the American Sociological Association, Chicago, III.

43. Kollmorgen, Walter M. (1991). The German-Swiss in Franklin Country, Tennessee: A Study of the significance of cultural considerations in Farming Enterprises, Washington, D. C., USDA B.A.E., Mimeo Bulletin.

44. Kroeber, A.L. (1923). Anthropology, N.Y., Harcourt Brace.

45. Kulkarni, S. D. (1975). Land Adivasi Story of the Peasants of Akkalkuya, EPW, Bombay.

46. Lerner, Daniel. (1958). The Passing of Traditional Society: Modernizing the Middle East, N.Y., The Free Press of Glencoe.

47. Lewis, D. S. (1991). Technologies and Transactions: a study of the interaction between new technology and agrarian structure in Bangladesh Dhaka: Centre for Social studies.

48. Lindstrom, Davin E. (1958). Diffusion of Agricultural and Home Economics Practices in Japanese Rural Community, in Rural Sociology, 23, 171-183.

49. Linton, Ralph. (1952). Cultural and Personality Factors Affecting Economic Growth, in Bert F. Hoselize (ed.) The Progress of Under-developed Areas, Chicago, University of Chicago Press.

50. Lionberger H.F. (1965). Some Implications from Diffusion Research for the Adoption of Farm Practices in India, Indian Journal of Extension Education, 1:18-25.

51. Loves, George J. (1955). A Description of Educational Practice in Metropolitan School Study Council Systems in 1954: With Special Reference to Elementary Schools, Ph. D. Thesis, N. Y., Columbia University Teachers College.

52. Mathur, P. N., K. N. Singh, and M. R. Lokhande. (1974). Source Utilization and Rate of Spread of Information on High Yielding Varieties of Wheat in a Farming Community. Indian Journal of Extension Education, 10 : 23-9.

53. Melnerney, J. P. (1978). The technology of rural development, World Bank Staff working paper 210, Washington, DC: World Bank.

54. Mort, Paul R. and Frances G. Cornell. (1941). American Schools in Transition, N. Y. Bureau of Publications, Teachers College, Columbia University.

55. Mosher, Arther T. (1966). Getting Agricultural Merits: Essential for Development and Modernization, New York, Praeger.

56. Mular, S. and R. N. Roy. (1968). Characteristics of Improved Farm Practices as Related to Adoption. Indian Journal of Extension Education, 4 : 40-8.

57. Pachori, R. S. and S. G. Tripathi. (1983). Impact of Intensive Agriculture Extention and Research Programme on Farmer's Knowledge of Technology', Indian Journal of Extention Education, 19: 72-3.

58. Parulekar, Godavari. (1975). Advisasis Revolt: The story of Warli Peasant in Struggle. National Book Agency Private Ltd., Bombay.

59. Patel, K. F. and D. N. Pandey. (1973). Source of Information in Adoption of Massouri Paddy. Rural India 37 : 75-8.

60. Pembertion, H. Earl. (1936). The Curve of Cultural Diffusion Rate. American Sociological Review, 1 : 547-556.

61. Polson, Robert A and Agation P. Paul. (1955). The Influence of Isolation on the Acceptance of Technological Changes in the Dumaguete City Trade Area, Philippines, Silliman Journal, 2, 149-159.

62. Rao, V. (1958). Rural Reactions to Urbanization, Summary of Ph.D. Thesis, University of Bombay, Journal of University of Bombay, 36(4) : 120.

63. Raj, S. Arul and A. John Knigh. (1977). Influence of Farm Practice Attributes on Innovation-Decision Process, Indian Journal of Extension Education, 13: 1-5.

64. Ray G.L. (1975). Contact of Extension Officers with Different Sources of Agriculture Practices in Andhra Pradesh, Indian Journal of Education, 11:65-6.

65. Reddy, S. K. and D. Rama Murthy. (1973). Impact of Functional Literacy on Agricultural Development. Indian Journal of Adult Education, 34: 18-20.

66. Redfield, Robert. (1947). "Cultural Change in Yucatan", in Nature and the Study of Society; edited by M. P. Redfield, Illinois: The University of Chicago Press.

67. Redclift, M. (1983). Production Programmes for Small Farmers: plan Ruebla as myth and reality Economic Development And Cultural Change, 31 PP. 551-570.

68. Rogers, Everett M. (1962). Diffusion of Innovation, New York: The Free Press of Glencoe. London: Macmillan New York.

69. Ross, Donald H. (1958). Administration for Adaptability: A Source Book Drawing Together the Results of More Than 150 Individual Studies Related to the Question of why and how Schools Improve, N. Y., Metropolitan School Study Council.

70. Rudra, Asok. (1987). Technology choice in agriculture in India over the past three decades. In Stewart, F. (ed.) Macro-Policies for Appropriate Technology in Developing Countries. Boulder, Co: Westview Press, PP. 22-73.

71. Ryan, Bryce and Neal C. Gross. (1943). The Diffusion of Hybrid Seed Grow in Communication and Change

in the Developing Countries, edited by Daniel Lerner and Wilbur Schramm Honolulu: East-West Centre Press.

72. Ryan. J. G. (1984). Efficiency and equality consideration in the design of agricultural technology in developing countries in Australian Journal of Agricultural Economics, 28 PP. 109-15.

73. Sahi, P. V. and M. D. Pawar. (1966). Farm Practice Attributes in Relation to Adoption, Indian Journal of Extention Education, 2: 136-46.

74. Sharp, Laurision. (1952). Steel Axes for Stone Age Australians, in Edward H. Spicer (ed.) Human Problems in Technological Change, N.Y., Russell Sage Foundation.

75. Singh, K. N., R. P. Singh and A. P. Mishra. (1971). Sources of Information Used in Relation to the Characteristics of the Users, Indian Journal of Adult Education, 32 : 3-8.

76. Singh, T. R. and S. N. Singh. (1980). Differential Perception of the Characteristics of Innovations of Farming Couples for HYV of Wheat and Family Planning Practices, Indian Journal of Extention Education, 6 : 16-21.

77. Singh, Y. P. and V. K. Babu. (1968). A Study of Adoption of Improved Farm Practices as a Function of Positive Values. Indian Journal of Extention Education, 4: 10-7.

78. Supe, S. V. (1971). Farmers' Information Sources Credibility and its Reduction to Their Rational and Adoption Behaviour, Indian Journal of Extention Education, 7: 29-33.

79. Schmidt W. (1939). The Culture Historical Method of Ethnology, translated S.A. Sicbu, P. 153.

80. Trade, Gabriel. (1903). The Laws of Imitation (trans. Clews Person), N.Y., Holt, Tinehart & Winston.

81. Wilrening, E.A. and others. (1960). Use and Role of Information Source among Dairy Farmers of Northern Victoria, Paper presented at the Rural Sociological Society, University Park, Penn.

82. Wissler, Clark. (1923). Man and Culture, N.Y., Growell.

❑❑❑

Index